Reputational Risk

A question of trust

Derek Atkins, Ian Bates, Lynn Drennan

institute of
financial services
School of Finance

airmic

LES50NS
PROFESS
PUBLIS

irm

BCI

D1293691

THE RISK MANAGEMENT ASSOCIATION
Serving the Financial Services Industry

institute of
Business Ethics
be

LES50NS PROFESSIONAL PUBLISHING Limited
A Division of LES50NS (PUBLISHING) Limited
Fitzroy House
11 Chenies Street
London WC1E 7EY
United Kingdom

Email: info@fiftylessons.com

Printed by Loupe Solutions

© LES50NS (PUBLISHING) Limited 2006

ISBN 0-85297-763-8

Foreword

Throughout our varied careers in the City of London, consultancy and academia each of us has often wondered why so many companies behave as they do, in apparent disregard for their reputations. Their behaviour is often very different from the way in which the individual managers conduct themselves in their personal lives.

Do some executives change into different people when they leave home in the morning for the office, only to change back again on their return in the evening? Alternatively, is there something about corporate life, especially in larger organisations, that creates a different perspective on the world?

All this came to a head following the turn of the millennium, when we witnessed the turmoil in business life, the collapse of the e-bubble and the long bull market, and a series of corporate scandals and failures such as Enron, WorldCom, Parmalat, Marconi and HIH. As a result, we felt that surely every senior executive must now, more than ever, be aware of how easily the reputation of even the greatest organisations can be damaged and their future viability threatened.

With this as our starting point, we decided to look deeper into the subject of reputational risk and what people have been thinking and saying about it, both inside and outside companies, and tried to reconcile this with our own practical experience. This led us on a fascinating journey, meeting business leaders, consultants, risk managers, academics, ethicists and many others. Gradually we began to piece together a picture of one of the most important corporate risks, but one which is seldom managed in a systematic manner. In other words, management had the responsibility without the control.

We originally envisaged writing a series of articles for the specialist risk management audience. However, we soon realised that we had an important message for senior management, and CEOs in particular. The result is this book, which is intended to raise the awareness of the importance of reputational risk, highlight some of the best practices in its management and give our own suggestions as to how reputational risk management might be further developed.

It is important to remember that the reputational risk considerations raised in this book are applicable to just about any type of organisation, not just corporate entities. Throughout this book we sometimes use the terms corporate and company when discussing the impact of reputational risk. However, all types of organisation, whether they be companies, charities, governmental functions and bodies, service providers such as schools and hospitals, or even political parties, are dependent on their reputation for their future success.

We hope you will find this book both informative and challenging, and that it may stimulate you to introduce some of the ideas it contains in your own organisation.

Derek Atkins, Ian Bates, Lynn Drennan

2006

Acknowledgements

We are endebted to a large number of experts in reputational risk, who willingly gave us their time and advice, while writing this book. It is not possible to list them all, but we would like to give especial thanks to David Gamble (AIRMIC), Julia Graham (BCI), David Brotzen (Brotzen Mayne), Oliver Prior (Willis), David Abraham (Marsh), Alex Marples (Kaisen), Simon Webley (IBE) and Bruce Nixon.

Disclaimer

Contents

Executive summary

Reputation is intangible, yet it is real enough to represent a significant element in the valuation of a company's shares. This 'reputational equity' may be several times the value of the tangible assets in companies with good reputations. Conversely, a company with a poor reputation can have negative reputational equity where the company is valued at less than the value of its tangible assets.

Reputational damage is consequently one of the most important risks any organisation faces. It is one of the few threats that can destroy an organisation as a viable concern. As the CEO of Coca Cola has made plain, he could lose all his factories and trucks and still rebuild his business, but if he lost his good name the company would be finished.

In the light of such sentiment, it is strange that very few companies or other organisations attempt to manage the risk to their reputation in a manner that is commensurate with its potential impact. This is despite the fact that corporate governance rules require listed companies to identify all their major risks and introduce appropriate control procedures to manage them. On the one hand, senior executives consistently nominate reputational loss in their top two most serious risks and, on the other hand, very few organisations allocate appropriate management effort to address it. This is the paradox that we set out to examine in this book.

In the first chapter we attempt to show why reputational risk is so complex, how it cuts across most existing management processes, and how responsibility for addressing it ends up, by default, with the CEO (though often not formally acknowledged). We describe how it can arise from any part of an organisation's activities and, although it takes many years to build a 'good' reputation, it can collapse rapidly, like a house of cards.

One of the problems we found in researching the published literature on reputational risk was a lack of consistency of approach. Some writers, for example, regarded reputation as being identical to brand, or in some cases even a sub-set of brand, others had a much wider perspective. As a result, we have developed what we believe to be a new, comprehensive, and hopefully robust, definition of reputational risk. By including the expectations of all stakeholders and referring to failure in both performance and behaviour, we believe that we have improved the understanding of this risk and given clues as to how it might be better controlled.

In the second chapter, we discuss the stakeholder model in some detail. We make no apologies for this. Having been early implementers of the model, the authors were convinced of its relevance to the long-term success of a company. However, for most of the intervening years, the stakeholder model, and its close companion CSR, have been largely considered an interesting indulgence while management got on with 'the real job' of maximising short-term shareholder value.

Attitudes are of course beginning to change, helped in no small measure by the fundamental change in the corporate landscape with the collapse of the long bull market and the 'e-bubble', together with a string of well publicised corporate frauds and failures. In this climate, a better understanding of reputational risk might well encourage even the most short-term, profit obsessed companies to take a broader perspective of their position in society. And, as a result, perhaps more might conclude that ethical business is good business after all.

In the third chapter we look at both performance and behavioural management. It is no accident that most company metrics are largely financial measures, often based on very short-term targets, as internal reporting reflects what management feel is expected of them. Again, a better understanding of reputational risk might well encourage a shift to a more holistic approach to management reporting. Reputational risk control requires companies to pay substantially more attention to non-financial and behavioural metrics, possibly along the lines of a form of balanced scorecard.

It is also clear to most observers that, apart from those of investors (and sometimes customers), stakeholder expectations are increasingly focused on how the company performs and behaves in relation to society or the environment, either just locally to its operations or in the wider world. A company's reputation can therefore be significantly damaged if these wider expectations are not met. Acting as a 'good corporate citizen' is increasingly not optional – it is required. The latest developments in UK governance and reporting requirements will specifically require that companies acknowledge and consider how they address a wide range of stakeholder expectations, and how they manage such issues as reputation, environmental and ethical risks, and report appropriately on them.

The fourth chapter looks at problems presented by a conventional risk management approach when trying to deal with reputational risk, and the work of risk consultants like Aon, Marsh and Willis to promote the concept of Active Reputational Risk Management. Whilst the consultants mainly come from the insurance broking community, the insurance solutions for reputational risk management are limited, and the focus is necessarily on risk management rather than risk transfer. Their research has shown that client companies tend to focus on post-event reputational risk management, with pre-event management often being regarded as too complex. While the consultants' methodologies may differ, they all promote a more systematic approach to reputational risk management and encourage clients to manage the risk proactively.

In the fifth chapter we draw together the ideas of these consultants and seek to apply the lessons and thinking developed earlier in this book, in order to propose a best practice model for reputational risk management. Key aspects of this model include the new definition of reputational risk to help clarify thinking; the need for the CEO to formally assume 'ownership' of the organisation's reputation; responsibility for reputational risk management to be formally allocated to a senior executive; and for it to be managed across the business as a single risk. By the CEO positively assuming ownership and by formally allocating responsibility in this way, a company can overcome the fragmentation that normally complicates this issue.

The management of reputational risk must also be entirely consistent with the achievement of the organisation's strategic objectives (this may mean adjusting those objectives once a full understanding of reputational risk has been obtained) and integrated with other risk management activity. But to manage it effectively it also needs to be owned, analysed and evaluated separately.

In the final chapter we look at three real life examples and the lessons that can be learned from them. And in the Appendices, we give practical suggestions and guidance on how our model for an effective reputational risk management process could be implemented.

You may well be asking, 'Is this too bureaucratic?' We believe that it is not unreasonable. After all, reputational risk is one of the most serious issues a management team will ever encounter, and regulators, corporate governance codes and future corporate reporting requirements require that it is being managed in a positive and effective way, alongside all other risks faced by the business.

Perhaps the question you should ask yourself, having read this book is:

'Could my organisation clearly demonstrate to a third party such as its external auditors that it is managing the entirety of its reputational risk in a positive and effective manner?'

Chapter 1

The importance of corporate reputation

On completing this chapter you will have begun to build an understanding as to why:

◆ whilst reputation is intangible, it is potentially an enormous asset;
◆ reputation is a wider concept than brand;
◆ reputation takes years to build up, but can be destroyed overnight;
◆ reputational risk can arise from any part of the organisation;
◆ current management of reputational risk tends to be fragmented, unsystematic and incomplete.

What is reputational risk?

As an organisation, how much do you value your reputation? It is totally intangible, yet it is likely to be critical for your continuing success.

❝❝ Reputation is an asset just as real as our people and brands. ❞❞

Joint-Chairmens' statement in the Introduction to Unilever's Code of Business Principles

The Chief Executive of Coca Cola went even further, saying

❝❝ If I lost all of my factories and trucks but kept the name Coca Cola, I could rebuild my business. If I lost my name, the business would collapse. ❞❞

Reputation is the most important commercial mechanism for conveying information to consumers.

John Kay, Foundations of Corporate Success, OUP 1993

Researchers such as Rory Knight and Deborah Pretty of Oxford Metrica have developed the concept of 'reputational equity' as a starting point for assessing the financial value for the reputation of a company. The underlying logic of this is described below.

Reputational equity

A significant part of many successful companies' share price is made up not from tangible assets such as property, stock and reserves, but from the goodwill element. This includes various intangibles such as the potential future profit stream, the value of brands, but above all it is a factor of a company's reputation. Any loss of reputation with one stakeholder group can spread to others and damage the company by erosion of what can be called reputational equity. Serious incidents or issues that cause major reputational damage can threaten a company's future results, even its existence. Paradoxically, if an incident or issue is perceived to be well handled by the company, recovery can be complete and, in rare cases, reputations have actually been enhanced.

It is important that a company understands the value of its reputation as to some extent this is a measure of the risk it is running. The greater the reputational contribution to the share price, the more there is to lose. For some well known companies the value of the reputation is several times that of their tangible assets.

Reputational damage is a major threat to a business

Damage to reputation can be disastrous, a fact which is clearly recognised by many senior executives. The insurance broker and risk consultant Aon, in its periodic survey of the senior executives of large companies, regularly has reputational risk at or near the top of the list of the greatest perceived threats to their businesses. The top ten greatest threats to business in the 2002-3 survey were ranked as follows:

1. Business interruption
2. **Loss of reputation**
3. Product liability/tamper/brand protection
4. Physical damage
5. General liability

6. Employee accidents
7. Failure to change/adapt
8. Environmental pollution
9. Professional indemnity
10. Failure of a key strategic alliance

It is interesting to note that *all* the other nine threats listed also represent threats to an organisation's reputation, ie they are each potential causes of reputational risk.

The paradox to this expression of concern by senior executives is that few organisations would appear to manage their reputation in a way that reflects its perceived significance – management has responsibility for the company's reputation, but lacks appropriate control.

In this book, we explore the special nature of reputational risk, explain why it is often managed in a fragmentary manner, and suggest how it might be dealt with more systematically. We specifically attempt to steer the reader away from the 'tick box' approach that appears to pervade so much risk management activity in the current business climate. As a report by the think tank Tomorrow's Company made plain, success in any activity that is done, at least partly, to meet the expectations of external stakeholders, requires positive conviction rather than a passive, box-ticking compliance mentality.

Positive conviction is needed to satisfy stakeholders' expectations

Much work to date, in the area of reputation management, has focused on the management of large, usually publicly-quoted, companies' reputations, particularly following significant events, such as disasters or accidents. It is important to remember, however, that all kinds of organisations, whether they be companies, charities, governmental functions and bodies, service providers such as schools and hospitals, or even political parties, are dependent on their reputation for their future success. Reputational risk management therefore should concern the executives of all types of organisations, not just quoted companies. In this book, we use the term organisation and company almost interchangeably except where we discuss the issues of share prices and investors and investment markets. As a rule, all concepts that we discuss apply equally well to all other types of organisation.

Why is reputation important?

An organisation's 'reputation' is the general estimation in which an organisation is held by the public and other observers, based on what is known or said about it.

Reputation versus brand

For the purposes of this book, we distinguish between the concepts of brand and reputation as follows.

◆ Brand is the intangible asset associated with the expected experience in a customer's mind when they deal with a company (product, presentation, quality, advertising style, customer service, etc). Trust in just that specific brand is lost when a brand is damaged.

◆ Reputation takes in the perspective of all stakeholders regarding all aspects of a company's performance or behaviour. Trust in the entire company is lost when reputation is damaged.

As an example, companies such as Unilever or Diageo own a wide range of separate and distinct consumer brands which, in the customers' eyes, are not linked to each other, or directly connected with the corporate name or reputation.

A brand can incorporate some of the factors that influence reputation (eg trust, fairness in dealing), and a company's reputation (with all stakeholders) can be harmed by damage to its brands, but this is just one of many potential causes of damage to a company's reputation.

Brand v Reputation

❝❝ We run a number of brands as a result of customer choice. However, having them does have the advantage of distancing the group's corporate reputation from damage that might occur in a subsidiary. ❞❞

Corporate Communications Director, major conglomerate

Reputation is much more than brand

Reputation is much more than the brand image, and includes factors such as trust in the organisation's integrity and how it will conduct itself in the future, both at the corporate level and through the actions of its management and staff. Different stakeholders may have varying, even conflicting, views on what they expect from the organisation. These differences can be quite significant, as we will examine later.

The information on which groups and individuals base their assessment of an organisation, and form an opinion on its reputation is, not surprisingly, usually incomplete. The end result is a general 'impression' which, nonetheless, will influence stakeholders' interactions with the company. Thus, favourable or unfavourable views of an organisation create a 'general impression halo' that may be either beneficial or detrimental to the organisation.

The importance of perception and the need to build reputational credit

❝ Reputation risk management differs from traditional risk management in an important respect: reputation is largely about perception. Many management teams have been criticised for the way they handled a crisis - not because their strategy was ill conceived or clumsily implemented, but because they failed to tell the outside world what the strategy was.

The way a company handles a crisis is not only dependent on the quality and timeliness of its decision-making, but also on how it is perceived by its stakeholders. This is based on a blend of perceptions, which may pre-date the crisis. If a company has a reputation for putting profit before principle, it will face a tougher battle to protect its reputation. Companies that weather crises of reputation have often accumulated "credit in the bank" with the public and stakeholders. ❞

Brotzen Mayne

A generally positive 'halo' may help an organisation protect its reputation, longer than may be warranted, during difficult times. On the other hand, a company possessing a more negative 'halo' will find that they do not have the benefit of the doubt, when things appear to go wrong. Such organisations are often described in the media as 'troubled', and minor events that might normally go unreported give rise to the opportunity for old stories to be revived and adverse publicity to continue. This creates a vicious circle, from which the organisation may find it difficult to break free.

A poor reputation creates a vicious circle

The power of talk

In his best selling book, 'The Tipping Point', Malcolm Gladwell describes how ideas or social trends may spread by word of mouth extremely rapidly, in a similar way to a virus spreading a contagious disease. This may help explain why reputations can be enhanced or damaged not only by big media disclosures but merely by people telling their friends. As with an epidemic, there may be a moment when a small change, a tipping point, causes society's interest in a particular issue/story/product to suddenly take off explosively.

For example, a company might have a history of behaving poorly in some particular area, but this may have very little impact on its public image. Then, one day, someone with a wide circle of influence (eg a journalist) has an unfortunate experience or has the matter brought to their attention. From that moment the 'news' can spread by geometric progression and suddenly the company has a reputational crisis on its hands. Good news can spread in the same way. Explosive demand for a product can arise simply from the recommendation of an opinion former (eg a well-known TV cook commenting on her favourite ingredient or utensil).

Reputation can therefore be 'good' or 'bad', depending on whether the organisation's behaviour and performance generates a mainly positive, or a negative, response from these interested parties.

The value of a good reputation

A 'good' reputation is highly valuable and can benefit a company enormously.

Potentially, it can result in:

- ◆ banks being willing to supply loans on more favourable rates and terms;
- ◆ good employees being attracted to work for the organisation, and their services being retained;
- ◆ investors being more likely to place their capital in the firm;
- ◆ improvement in sales;
- ◆ maintenance and enhancement of market share;
- ◆ public perception of the organisation as an asset to the society in which it operates.

Like other assets, a good reputation can be leveraged for positive advantage.

In contrast, a poor reputation means that the company is vulnerable. It may find difficulty in attracting and retaining staff. Indeed, it is likely that good staff will leave at the earliest opportunity for an employer that offers better career prospects. Limits may be put on borrowing, with more stringent terms for repayment, and customers may decide to purchase their goods elsewhere, unless incentivised to stay (eg by price cuts).

It takes years to establish a good reputation – Ratner

A 'good' reputation often takes years of hard work to establish, but can be severely damaged very easily and very quickly. An extreme example was that of Gerald Ratner, the Chief Executive of one of the eponymous jewellery retailers in the UK. In a public address he made the flippant remark that one of the company's best selling products was 'total crap'. This received huge publicity and the company suffered severe damage to its reputation. Ratner was forced to resign and the company changed its name to Signet in order to survive.

Interestingly, Ratner subsequently tried to use the Ratner name in respect of an on-line jewellery e-tailer. Signet refused to allow the name to be used, arguing that its use by a competitor would cause confusion in the marketplace. Which would seem to confirm, at least Signet's belief, in the old adage that 'there's no such thing as bad publicity'.

The Ratner case demonstrates another aspect of reputational risk. As reputation is an external judgement made about the organisation, reputational damage is not limited to that caused by real events, but could arise out of misconceptions, rumours or even a director's tasteless joke.

Vulnerability of companies with high reputational equity

Where reputational equity makes up a substantial element of a company's value reputational damage can have a much greater impact on that company.

Alan Greenspan, Chairman of the US Federal Reserve Board, is quoted as saying "the rapidity of Enron's decline is an effective illustration of the vulnerability of a firm whose market value rests largely on a capitalised reputation. The physical assets of such a firm compose a small proportion of its asset base. Trust and reputation can vanish overnight. A factory in such a context cannot".

Arthur Andersen represents a similar case. As a professional services firm it traded on its reputation. The moment that reputation suffered serious damage, the company ceased to be a viable entity.

Size is no protection

 Size and success are no protection when things go wrong, indeed, the bigger the brand (or reputation), the bigger the risk.

Kate Hinsley, De La Rue, 2001

Andersen 'prays for a miracle'

Andersen's hopes of surviving as a pure auditing practice faded yesterday as fears grew that the accounting firm could make an unprecedented Chapter 11 bankruptcy filing.

Concern over Andersen's future came after Paul Volcker, the former Federal reserve Chairman who was hired to restructure the accounting firm, said that only a 'miracle' would turn the firm around.

It is thought that his plan to save Andersen, which would involve spinning off most of its consulting business to leave behind a core auditing practice has stalled at a crucial stage. This is because hardly any of the conditions that would have made Andersen's reorganisation possible have been met. These include Andersen's settlement of criminal and civil lawsuits related to Enron and a resolution to the Securities and Exchange Commission inquiry into the firm. Andersen is facing a criminal trial on May 6 over allegations that it obstructed justice in the Enron scandal.

Andersen's clients drift away

Clients reviewing their relationship:

Colgate Palmolive

Hershey

Costco

Clients already lost:

Federal Express

Freddie Mac

Delta Air Lines

Merck

Texaco

Sara Lee

*Extract from news item, **The Times**, 24 April 2002*

Once a company's reputation begins to fall, it is often the best customers who are the first to go elsewhere.

What are the sources of reputational risk?

Continuing with the premise that 'reputational equity' is a useful term to describe that element of a company's total 'value' represented by its intangible, rather than tangible assets, it is important to bear in mind that this assessment of value is not limited to purely monetary concepts (eg the value of brands or expectation of future profits). It incorporates a much broader concept of value, including 'value to society' and trust, which is then incorporated by shareholders into the share price. In some circumstances the value of reputational equity can be negative, and the company would then be valued at less than the value of its tangible assets.

Reputational equity can be influenced (either increased or decreased) by the performance and behaviour of the business components and the employees of the company, but it tends to be only subject to 'damage' from external events and changes, eg issues or events arising in other companies or markets, changes in law or regulation.

'Renting' a reputation

One means by which an organisation can enhance its reputation is by 'renting' the good reputation of another party. The hiring of celebrity or high profile directors is one way in which a company can seek to signal its worth and integrity to the capital markets and other stakeholders. The inference being that, if such a high profile individual is willing to have their name linked with the company, then it must have a good reputation. This type of appointment can be particularly valuable for smaller firms.

Likewise, it used to be suggested that companies could gain credibility for their financial statements by 'renting' the reputations of their external auditors, in whom investors were believed to place significant faith as to the reliability and quality of the accounting firm's audit process. However, with all of the (remaining) Big 4 accounting firms being the subject of lawsuits connected to their roles in a range of corporate failures, scandals or problems in the last few years, and Andersens collapsing as a result of such problems, this may not carry as much weight today.

Hurn to stand down as chairman of Prudential

Sir Roger Hurn said yesterday that he would quit his £300,000 a year job as chairman of Prudential, paying the price for his disastrous tenure in the same position at Marconi. Sir Roger said that he was concerned that the insurer would be damaged by his association with Marconi.

During his time at the embattled telecoms equipment provider, more than 13,000 workers lost their jobs and the company's stock market value crashed from a high of £35 billion to just £183 million. Sir Roger resigned last September after a boardroom putsch that saw him replaced by Derek Bonham.

Prudential insisted that it had not been under pressure from shareholders over Sir Roger's position. However, a number of institutions said they had been expecting action to be taken for some time. Robert Talbot, managing director of Royal & SunAlliance Investments said, 'Sir Roger appears to have paid the price of his association with Marconi. This highlights the problems for directors of reputational risk.'

*Extract from news item, **The Times**, 25 April 2002*

> *Senior executives and business leaders carry their personal reputations from job to job – this can be a double-edged sword. If they are viewed as successful, this will enhance the reputation of their current employer, but if their reputation suffers damage from issues relating to the past or other roles carried on in parallel, the employer may also be at risk of suffering damage to its reputation.*

In what ways can reputational risk impact the organisation?

As we have already suggested, reputational risk may take many forms. This is one reason why it is so difficult to manage in its entirety, and why much management action in respect of it is fragmentary. The following are a few examples of the diverse ways it might impact an organisation.

Reputational risk takes many forms

a) Products and services

The perception (whether valid or not) that an organisation's products or services are of poor quality or over-priced can destroy customer confidence and the organisation's sales and profitability. Recent examples include the following.

- ◆ **Perrier**: Accidental contamination of mineral water led to traces of benzene appearing in the product. This led to a world-wide product recall, which cost the company tens of millions of dollars in lost sales. Perrier were criticised for the way in which they handled the incident, including a delay in withdrawing the product from the shelves. The company faced a massive spend on re-packaging and advertising before they could re-launch the product, and it took several years before they were able to win back their market share. This incident is considered to have been instrumental in Perrier's later acquisition by Nestlé.
- ◆ **Arthur Andersen**: There was a dramatic loss of confidence in the quality of the professional services provided by this large accounting firm, resulting from the company's involvement with a number of firms (most notably Enron) that were embroiled in corporate financial scandals together with allegations of professional misconduct (document shredding) being made against the firm. The publicity surrounding these events, caused other major clients of Andersen's to desert them in droves, with the result that this long-established accountancy practice ceased to exist.

Perrier taken off the shelves worldwide

160 million bottles to be scrapped

All bottles of Perrier, the French mineral water, are to be withdrawn from sale worldwide after traces of benzene, a solvent which has been linked with cancer, were discovered in supplies of the drink in Britain and several other European countries.

Preliminary results showed low-level benzene contamination in bottled Perrier in Britain. Traces of benzene contamination were also discovered in samples in West Germany, Denmark and the Netherlands.

M Gustave Leven, president of Source Perrier, the French parent company, announced the withdrawal of all stocks of its famous 'designer' water yesterday at a press conference in Paris after the spread of the health scare from the United States, where the contamination was first discovered, to Europe.

The decision to dispose of some 160 million of the distinctive Indian-club shaped bottles at an estimated cost of £40 million was taken despite Perrier's insistence that the "infinitesimal" traces of toxic benzene discovered in supplies did not pose the slightest threat to consumers' health.

*Extract from news item, **The Times**, 15 February 1990*

This was particularly damaging as it struck at the core competence of a mineral water supplier, that is the purity and 'healthiness' of the product. It also demonstrates another aspect of risk. A problem does not need to exist in reality for reputation to be damaged. There needs only to be a public perception of a problem for the vicious circle to begin.

b)   Financial performance

A loss of trust from the investment community (analysts, fund managers, bankers, City editors, credit agencies) in the ability of a company to deliver acceptable returns, can dramatically affect share prices, the cost of borrowing or raising new equity capital, and may lead to pressure for fundamental change in the company. Recent examples include the following.

- ◆ **Vivendi-Universal**: The enforced change of chief executive and subsequent sell-off of recently acquired major business units following a disastrous acquisition programme, and the chief executive publicly stating that the company was 'in better than great shape', despite having made the largest loss ever made by a French company.
- ◆ **Marconi**: The enforced changes to senior management and corporate strategies following a disastrous change of strategic direction, a number of over-priced acquisitions, and the consistent failure of the management team to deliver on their promises. The creditors eventually took over 99.5% of the equity of the business.

15

c)   Executive performance

A belief that a company's senior managers are acting in a manner that places their personal interests and rewards ahead of those of any other stakeholders can lead to shareholder, employee or regulatory pressure for change in board structures and reward schemes. Examples include.

- ◆ **Skandia**: The Swedish insurance group announced, in December 2003, that it would prosecute its former chief executive, finance director and head of its life assurance company, for an alleged spend of 8m kroner of Skandia funds on the renovation of their luxury Stockholm apartments. An investigation into the company's corporate activities also criticised the bonus scheme which, in the three years preceding 2000, paid top executives a total of around 2bn kroner, (around £150m).
- ◆ **New York Stock Exchange**: The New York Public Prosecutor has launched a court case to seek to recover some of this non-profit organisation's retiring chief executive's final 'remuneration' which is reported to have exceeded $140m.
- ◆ The additional burden of corporate governance obligations (eg the US Sarbanes-Oxley Act, the UK Combined Code on Corporate Governance) that have been imposed as a reaction to the procession of corporate scandals, from Polly Peck, Maxwell and BCCI to Enron, Tyco, WorldCom and Parmalat.

d)   Unacceptable corporate behaviour

If an organisation is found to be acting in an unacceptable manner, or to have knowingly failed to comply with official rules, standards or laws, there will be a substantial loss of trust in how the organisation will behave in future, from investors, regulators/standards bodies and potentially customers. Questions will also be asked about the honesty, integrity and management capability of the entire senior management team and board of directors. For example.

- ◆ The aggressive 'promotion' of new share issues by investment analysts working for large investment banks, particularly of internet companies in the US in the late 1990s, for the benefit of existing customers and in the hope of gaining future investment banking fees, when it seems the analysts themselves did not believe in the shares. Several of the large US banks have had to pay a total of $1.4 billion in fines and penalties levied by the regulatory authorities, and class actions from investors who lost money as a result of such actions continue against a number of banks.

It is the same in Australia

The reputation of Corporate Australia has taken something of a battering flowing from the recent round of corporate collapses. On the evidence emerging, failure to observe, or a disregard for, good corporate governance practice and related internal control processes have been a significant contributing factor in not fully informing the market on the real state of affairs of these companies.

This has been amplified by other factors including the influence of powerful executives, apparent conflicts of interest and, more disturbing, suggestions of collusive behaviour.

Tom Pockett, National President, Group of 100,
AFR Conference on Corporate Governance, 2002

R&SA chief to get £1m payoff

Bob Mendelsohn, the American chief executive of Royal & SunAlliance, is set to fall on his sword with a £1 million-plus payoff as the price for ensuring the success of a crucial £800 million rights issue.

Bankers say R&SA is in the process of putting together 'a complete market solution' to deal with its battered finances and tattered reputation, including a rights issue to raise capital, a management restructuring and a pledge to exit unprofitable lines of business.

R&SA has repeatedly missed targets to lower its combined ratio, a measure of underwriting profitability, and faces unflattering comparisons with rivals in the sector, many of whom are beating internal profits targets.

*Extract from news item, **The Times**, 7 September 2002*

This interesting case provides lessons in handling corporate reputation:

Bob Mendelsohn used his undoubted inspirational leadership skills in an effort to restore the company's results in a notoriously volatile general insurance market. This involved him setting, and making public, his stretching targets for future operating ratios. When these were missed, he unfortunately had to pay the price of failing to meet the expectations that he had helped to create.

***Lesson 1**: Avoid creating hostages to fortune – try not to make what appear to be public promises unless you are absolutely sure your colleagues are going to deliver them. Institutional investors and the financial press are an unforgiving bunch.*

R&SA's reputation was further damaged as the media drew attention to the severance terms – implying that they were generous.

Lesson 2: Companies obviously must provide competitive packages to attract the best talent, but they need to be prepared for the fact that the media will usually interpret this, rightly or wrongly, as a reward for failure when meeting contractual rights on an executive's departure.

Fat cats

The question of executive remuneration is extremely controversial, and may have considerable impact on corporate reputation. On the one hand, large companies need to pay internationally competitive salaries to attract the best managerial talent. On the other hand, rewards sometimes appear to be out of proportion, especially when compared with staff salaries. This issue came to a head in the UK during the period of privatisation of utilities. The media focused on the high level of remuneration of some of the new utility company directors in comparison with their state sector predecessors. The term 'fat cat' entered the business vocabulary and has remained there ever since.

Any well-paid executive might be accused of being a fat cat, but particular criticism is levelled if the public or media believe that the company is unsuccessful and the executive is being 'rewarded for failure'. The reputational damage arises from a perception that management are putting their own interests ahead of those of the shareholders, customers and staff.

---

e) Employees

A loss of trust between the organisation's workforce and its management can lead to industrial action, poor morale, and may lead in some instances to a lack of quality in the products or services offered to customers. Examples include:

◆ **British Airways**: Significant flight cancellations and disruption in summer 2003, caused by staff walkouts at Heathrow following the introduction of a new electronic clocking-on system.
◆ A number of other high profile examples have resulted from attempts to 'modernise' or part-privatise what were previously seen as 'public services', funded and operated on behalf of local or central government in the UK. Examples include:
  ● The Fire Service;
  ● The Post Office;
  ● National Air Traffic Control.

f) Health and safety

A significant industrial accident, or incident involving members of the public, may damage the trust of employees, the community and government. This can lead to the involvement of external bodies, such as the Health and Safety Executive; to full investigation, by means of a public inquiry, on how the incident arose, and how similar situations might be prevented in future; and to civil and criminal proceedings, including the greater use of the charge of corporate manslaughter in the UK courts. Where an event is perceived to have been 'preventable' – particularly where previous warnings have been given, and these have been ignored or underestimated – then the reputation of the organisation responsible will be severely tarnished. The most recent significant examples, in the UK, have involved the railways (Paddington and Hatfield) but the issues apply just as much to companies in other sectors.

Major incidents

Large scale accidents such as the Three Mile Island (USA) and Chernobyl nuclear disasters (Russia), the Flixborough chemical explosion and the Kings Cross Underground Station fire (UK) have reputational implications well beyond those of the organisations immediately involved. Damage may be done to public trust in a whole industry and this might take many years to be restored. The toxic gas release from the Union Carbide plant in Bhopal is reputed to have killed 13,000 people in the neighbourhood and injured many more. The company paid several million dollars in damages at the time and has since been absorbed by Dow Corporation. One would expect that to be the end of the matter. However, twenty years on, the state government in India has reawakened its interest in the case leading the media to re-run criticisms of multinationals in general and the chemical industry in particular. The situation prompted one commentator to suggest that major incidents come under the jurisdiction of two different courts. First, there is a court of law that determines liability, awards damages and closes the case. The second is the court of public opinion and this may continue to make judgements for years to come.

g) Environment

Public engagement with environmental issues is at an all-time high. Everything from the situation of wind farms, mobile phone masts and waste incinerators, to the planting and use of genetically modified (GM) crops, the increase in air and water pollution, and government's efforts (or lack of them) in respect of domestic waste recycling, comes under immense media scrutiny. Local, national, and international pressure groups such as Friends of the Earth and Greenpeace, are adept at using the media to present their case, and often gain an advantage over those they are challenging, because they are more readily able to give the media the human interest story that they seek. Pressure groups may also benefit from the inherent distrust in which government and 'big business' is held. Examples include:

◆ **Exxon**: The repercussions of the Exxon Valdez oil spill of 1989 continue to rumble on. In January 2004, the company was ordered to pay $4.5bn in punitive damages to fishermen and others affected by the spill. Exxon is appealing the decision. Greenpeace dispute Exxon's argument that all impacted species in the area of the spill are on the road to recovery, if not fully recovered, and are urging a continuing boycott of Exxon, Mobil and Esso products.

◆ **Monsanto**: Despite its efforts to persuade the EU consumer that GM crops are safe, Monsanto announced in October 2003 that it was closing its European seed cereal business, in the UK, and closing down operations in France, Germany and the Czech Republic. The EU Environment Commissioner, Margot Wallstrom, said that US bio-tech companies were "trying to lie" and 'force' unsuitable GM technology onto Europe. Monsanto said the move was 'a strategic decision to realign the company's core businesses' but anti-GM campaigners said they believed the decision was related to the GM controversy in Europe.

◆ **Shell**: The company took the logical (and subsequently shown to be the most environmentally sound), but somewhat insensitive, decision to dispose of the Brent Spar oil platform by towing it out to sea and sinking it (and the hundreds of tons of waste oil and other hazardous chemicals that it contained) in the deep ocean. Greenpeace and other environmental campaigners fought a high profile, and eventually successful, campaign to stop disposal in this way. Shell suffered extensive negative publicity over several months as a result of this campaign, resulting in consumer boycotts at, and physical damage to some of its service stations.

h)   Customer relations

The widespread perception, whether valid or not, that a company is acting unfairly towards, or showing a lack of respect for, its customers may significantly damage sales and may, where relevant, encourage intervention from the regulatory authorities. This can happen in any industry (eg the Ratner case) but it is especially prevalent in the financial services sector where products are relatively intangible and can be long term in nature, meaning that their value or suitability may not be apparent until some years after the original purchase. Examples include.

◆ **The UK Life and Pensions Industry**: where the 'mis-selling' of personal pensions, and endowments, has led to accusations that financial services advisers were more interested in the commission they could earn from the product providers than in ensuring the financial needs of their clients were met. The involvement of the Insurance Ombudsman has allowed many aggrieved customers to successfully claim for some recompense, although in most cases this still does not amount to the expected value of the pension or endowment in question.

◆ **The major retail banks**: where the announcement of massive profits in 2004 has led to calls for improved service, lower charges and an end to outdated practices, such as the number of days that banks take to 'officially' clear a deposit transaction – a practice that allows them to benefit from investment interest, while denying the customer access to their money.

The speed and accessibility of the internet has increased the rate at which reputational risk can impact an organisation. The old saying 'news travels fast' was never so true as it is today. 'Bad' news – whether genuine or not – can rapidly get a global airing. Some websites have been established with the sole aim of providing a forum for criticism of a business or its product,

Bad news travels fast – even faster via the internet

and the larger the corporation, the more likely this is to occur, as Microsoft and McDonalds have found to their cost.

Own goal

The impulsive Mr Ratner miscalculated on the grand scale, perhaps thinking that a speech in the Albert Hall constituted a discreet private occasion. If his customers are tasteless they are surely not so stupid as to think they will now impress their peers or lift their own spirits by buying trinkets from Ratners. At the least, therefore, the entire Ratners chain might have to be rebranded.

Any corner shop owner knows you do not prosper by telling your customers you despise them. A deeper question is whether you can prosper in the long run if you despise them in private.

*Extract from 'Comment' column, **The Times**, 25 April 1991*

Senior executives should beware of making 'jokes' about their company's products. Not everyone may see the funny side – especially customers and shareholders.

The power of the internet

" The internet has opened up new areas of reputation risk, and caused old ones to proliferate. Corporate web sites are bastardised, companies discover pornography on their employees' workstations, and employees can be prosecuted for maligning competitors via e-mail. In addition, complainants can use the cheap, immediate power of the web to mobilise other supporters around the world. "

Brotzen Mayne

Vulnerability of companies where problems occur at the 'core' of the business

Any organisation could be severely damaged by financial irregularities, unfair treatment of customers or employees, a series of poor operating results, or a physical disaster, such as a major accident or explosion. However, companies appear to be most vulnerable to reputational loss if the problem relates directly to what stakeholders perceive to be one of their core areas of competence or responsibility. Stakeholders will tend to take the view that if such a core area to the business is not managed effectively, then the business as a whole does not warrant the stakeholders' trust.

21

For example, a motor manufacturer might have a minor fire at a factory and suffer minimal reputational damage. A chemical company experiencing a similar incident is likely to fare much worse, as the consequences of such an incident may be more severe, and therefore expectations of safety will be much higher.

Different causes, different expectations

As we have seen, companies are exposed to reputational risk from a wide range of threats that can either build up gradually, or occur suddenly. Looking at the examples above, we can reasonably conclude the following.

- ◆ Different stakeholders can, and do, have different expectations of what they want from the organisation in terms of both its performance (financial and non-financial) and its behaviour.
- ◆ The potential for reputational damage has many causes. They can emanate from any part of the business. They can be initiated by the actions of a single employee, a small group of employees, or the behaviour of the organisation as a whole, or can be the result of external pressures or events.
- ◆ Companies appear to be most vulnerable to reputational damage if a problem arises that relates to what third parties view as one of the company's core areas of competence.

This diversity explains both why the risk is perceived to be so high, and why it can be difficult to manage.

Think the unthinkable

❝❝ Risk managers are increasingly accepting that the unthinkable can happen, and it cannot necessarily be insured

David Gamble, AIRMIC, 2003

Reputational risk: a new definition

The challenge posed in managing reputational risk becomes a little clearer when one tries to define the concept more specifically. We propose the following definition:

Reputational risk = **Failure to meet stakeholders' reasonable expectations of an organisation's performance *and* behaviour.**

This is a far broader definition than some other commentators have provided, where reputation is linked – quite often only as a sub-set – to brand, without consideration of some of the much wider implications of reputational damage that we have discussed above.

Why just 'reasonable' expectations?

Some commentators would suggest that a company must also understand and be prepared to manage the 'unreasonable' expectations of stakeholders. Without getting too involved in semantics, we accept the proposition that companies need to understand all stakeholder expectations, both reasonable and unreasonable; however, it is then a judgement call for management to decide how the company attempts to meet any specific expectation. A conscious decision not to address specific stakeholders' expectations will need to be risk managed in the same way as any other identified risk to the company.

In practice, however, a failure to meet what is generally felt to be an unreasonable expectation of the company is unlikely to have a significant impact on the company's reputation.

In most large organisations, reputational risk, as we have defined it, is most unlikely to be allocated as the responsibility of a single person other than, by default, the chief executive. There is also a general impression that, in the past, non-executive directors may have been unwilling to challenge the executive directors on how the company's reputation is managed as a separate and valuable business asset, for fear of being seen as disloyal. So, unless it is specifically brought up by an executive, or forced onto the agenda through having to deal with a crisis, most boards have had a tendency to avoid discussing reputational risk as a separate and significant business issue.

Reputation is seldom discussed as a separate business issue

Moreover, where it has been looked at to any extent, it is quickly discovered to be complex, hard to measure and not easy to control. Thus in the majority of cases:

◆ Reputational risk is 'managed' on a day-to-day basis in a highly fragmentary manner, with various causes of reputational risk being managed independently under different risk management sub-plans (eg Health and Safety, HR practices, Product Quality, Corporate Relations/Investor Management).

◆ The only clearly visible element of reputational risk management tends to be reactive, post-event crisis management, (rather than a proactive, holistic risk management process which includes preventive and other pre-event risk mitigation actions).

This is essentially because:

◆ The expectations of all of the various stakeholder groups have not been consistently ascertained and codified. As a result, it is unlikely that considered decisions on how the organisation wishes to specifically respond to each of those expectations will be made or communicated to all relevant parties.

◆ All the potential causes of reputational risk have not been clearly identified, assessed and linked together logically within the existing risk management framework.

As a result, we believe that most organisations, currently do not manage their reputational risk in a manner that is systematic, effective, or allows them to form an overall assessment of the gross risk faced. Nor are they in a position to assess the residual risk that the company is exposed to, after taking into account the risk management activity currently performed. Potentially therefore, such organisations are in breach of the UK Combined Code requirements to establish an effective system of internal control based on a sound understanding of the risks faced by the organisation.

Using our definition of reputational risk as a starting point, we have attempted to group together the main methods a company might use to manage elements of it. Most companies use some of them, a minority use all of them, but very few take a holistic approach to the issue.

1. Stakeholders' reasonable expectations

Addressing reputational risk from the perspective of the stakeholders' expectations tends to primarily involve the corporate strategy and corporate communications/PR functions of a company. Between them they should be maintaining a constructive and continuous relationship with all key stakeholders, to ensure that their expectations are understood, and that the company's strategy, plans and performance are kept in reasonable alignment with those expectations.

This might appear an obvious requirement, but unfortunately many businesses look little beyond the short-term needs of their shareholders and (for those who claim

Simplified diagram of how most companies currently appear to 'manage' reputational risk

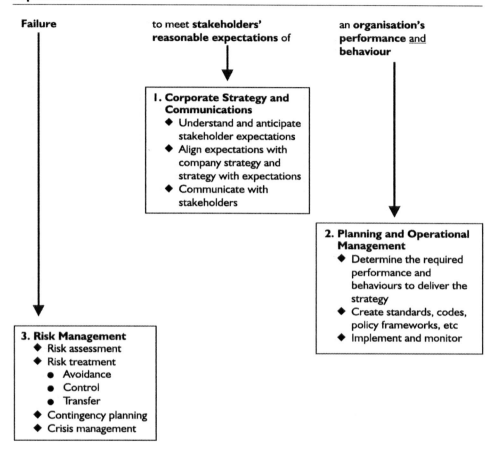

Failure ──────── to meet **stakeholders' reasonable expectations** of ──────── an **organisation's performance <u>and</u> behaviour**

1. Corporate Strategy and Communications
- ◆ Understand and anticipate stakeholder expectations
- ◆ Align expectations with company strategy and strategy with expectations
- ◆ Communicate with stakeholders

2. Planning and Operational Management
- ◆ Determine the required performance and behaviours to deliver the strategy
- ◆ Create standards, codes, policy frameworks, etc
- ◆ Implement and monitor

3. Risk Management
- ◆ Risk assessment
- ◆ Risk treatment
  - ● Avoidance
  - ● Control
  - ● Transfer
- ◆ Contingency planning
- ◆ Crisis management

to be 'customer-focused') their customers, and regard meeting the expectations of employees, business partners, government and regulators, the public and others as largely incidental.

2. The organisation's performance and behaviour

These are the realms of planning and operational management. Performance management, that is the setting of standards, codes, policy frameworks and the like, then implementation of them, and monitoring to ensure appropriate performance, should represent a core activity for any company. The fact that there is increasing intervention by regulators and standards setters suggests that all is not well everywhere. Moreover, the parallel management of behaviour, through the development, embedding and monitoring of ethical and behavioural codes has a tendency to be either overlooked or, at best, only paid lip service in many companies. There are many examples of companies where formal behavioural codes have been produced, but there has been no serious attempt made to ensure compliance with them, nor to ensure that the underlying culture or business targets and incentive schemes are consistent with the code.

3.   Failure

The focus on failure understandably epitomises the approach taken by a risk management function in a company. Risks that have potential implications for reputation are identified, assessed and decisions made on the best way of handling them. This may include contingency planning and post-loss crisis management planning. Some excellent work is done in this area, especially where it has been inspired by the major insurance brokers. Nevertheless, too often companies concentrate on the traditional list of physical disasters and miss the wider spectrum of risks and issues which we have outlined earlier.

Conclusion

A company's reputation can have either a positive or a negative impact on its success. To ensure that this impact is positive, the causes of reputational risk need to be proactively identified, assessed and managed. Since reputational risk can arise from many different sources, its comprehensive management will necessitate the involvement of a range of different functions within the company.

In the next chapter, we will examine the stakeholder model in relation to corporate reputation, and discuss the expectations of a range of stakeholders, in both the short and long term, and how this may impact on reputation and reputational risk management.

Chapter 2

Stakeholder expectations

On completing this chapter you will have begun to build an understanding as to why:

◆ each of the stakeholder groups has different expectations of the organisation;
◆ the expectations of shareholders, employees, customers, business partners, government/regulators, the general public and NGOs of the organisation may sometimes conflict;
◆ there is a systemic short-termism in business due to companies focusing on the perceived short-term expectations of shareholders and investment markets;
◆ focusing on any stakeholder group at the expense of the others creates reputational risk.

What do stakeholders really want?

In the first chapter of this book we looked at the nature of, and some of the challenges faced in managing, reputational risk in general. In this second chapter, we examine issues presented by the range of stakeholders in a company, and the different expectations they may have of the company's performance and behaviour.

Shareholder value maximisation

 It is only over the last 20 years that the doctrine has been born that companies are solely in business to maximise shareholder value and devil take the hindmost.

Roger Cowe, No Scruples

The stakeholder model

In the early 1990s we were closely involved in helping develop a new strategic direction for a leading FTSE 100 company. The overall objective was to fulfil defined shareholder expectations but the novel approach was the use of a stakeholder model. The executive board accepted that its prime responsibility was to the long-term interests of the shareholders, as owners. However, they also accepted that, to ensure the long-term viability of the business, the reasonable expectations of the other key stakeholder groups needed to be satisfied as well.

The basic proposition of the stakeholder model is that a business has a range of different 'stakeholders' who each have an interest in the company, its behaviour and performance, and whose **Stakeholders have** needs and expectations of the company vary. The theory **different interests** behind this model is that the management of a company are essentially trustees of the company's resources, and are responsible for allocating them in an appropriate and effective manner to satisfy the needs and expectations of the various stakeholders.

The stakeholder model

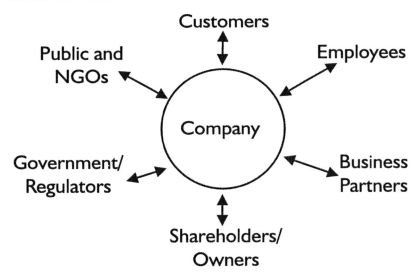

At the time, this broad-based and long-term view of the role of a company was considered to be highly radical and generated considerable interest both within and outside the organisation. Unfortunately, the full results of this strategy were never known, as the company became involved in a merger, and the new entity adopted a completely different strategy.

The multiple stakeholder model, and increasing obligations under the generic title of Corporate Social Responsibility (CSR), are now more commonly used to influence corporate strategy development. By 1999 a UK government committee of inquiry under the title, 'A New Vision for Business' was recommending that companies should be promoting the stakeholder model so 'enhancing shareholders' interests by simultaneously meeting wider ethical, social and environmental responsibilities'.

Attitudes towards the stakeholder model

There is a spectrum of attitudes towards the stakeholder model, which can be summarised as follows.

1. The shareholder is the primary focus of the company's attention and creating shareholder value is the overwhelming purpose. Obligations to all other stakeholders are totally subservient to meeting shareholder expectations.

2. The shareholder is the prime focus, but this is tempered by the belief that the creation of long-term shareholder value can only be ensured by satisfying the needs of the other stakeholders over the long term as well.

3. Companies acknowledge that they are responsible to society as a whole and they must look to meet the needs and expectations of the entire breadth of society. Shareholders are merely one section of society and have equal priority with all other sections.

The first position, where the shareholder is the be-all and end-all of a company's existence is, theoretically, totally valid. However, increasingly, society's expectations are much greater than this, and the company would be running a significant reputational risk to maintain such an extreme position, other than in the short term.

It is interesting to note that, when incorporation of companies was introduced two centuries ago it was on the assumption that companies had an economic and societal purpose. The government was effectively giving them a 'licence to trade'. Profit and limited liability were the rewards for fulfilling this important role and for increasing the prosperity of the nation as a whole.

There have always been bad employers – the need for an active trade union movement is a living testimony to their existence – however, the obsession with short-term shareholder value maximisation, with its associated tunnel vision and neglect for other stakeholders, appears to be a fairly recent phenomenon. Shareholders may be happy with it (at least in the short term) but, increasingly, the public at large and many influential special interest groups are not.

Stakeholder relationships

" The idea that a firm may have responsibilities beyond those owed to the shareholders appears obvious to some people but totally alien to others. "

Risk Management Consultant

" The control of the great corporations should develop into a purely neutral technocracy balancing a variety of claims by various groups in the community and assigning to each a portion of the income stream on the basis of public policy rather than private cupidity. Corporations would likely have to embrace this new approach if the corporate system was to survive. "

Adolf Berle, Gardiner Means
The Modern Corporation and Private Property, Harcourt Brace, 1968

" Management are responsible for satisfying the needs of the various stakeholders, and managing what should be six mutually beneficial relationships. It is a bit like the old circus act where you have to keep six plates spinning on the top of six different poles all at the same time. "

CEO, major UK company

" All international businesses face increasing scrutiny from consumers, investors, employees, governments, non-governmental organisations and the media. These groups have widely differing agendas. The anti-globalisation movement attacks large corporations in the belief that modern capitalism undermines local communities and local economies. Consumers and ethical fund managers boycott companies for wrong-doing or lack of ethical standards and trading partners demand that suppliers conform with their business principles. In this climate, the reputation of Unilever is constantly being scrutinised if it is not actually under attack. "

Unilever

" If companies are no longer prepared to accept that they have a societal purpose (ie to act in a way that is beneficial to a range of stakeholders, not just their shareholders), society may be justified in no longer granting them limited liability. "

Roger Steare

The challenge of short termism

Why is business, particularly in the Anglo-Saxon world, so short termist? Short termism is undoubtedly one of the greatest threats to reputation, as it distorts corporate priorities. As Lawrence Mitchell wrote in his book Corporate Irresponsibility:

> 'Corporations are often so focused on making short term profits for their stockholders that they behave in ways that adversely affect their employees, the environment, consumers, American politics, and even the long term well being of the corporation.'

It seems to be a systemic problem. There is an oversupply of investment opportunities, so companies must compete for the attention of well-informed and demanding shareholders. The long bull market of the last twenty or so years of the 20th century did not help. Unrealistic expectations (the new paradigm) of never-ending growth and high returns were created. As a consequence, the pressure on senior executives is immense: appear to perform, and do it quickly – or you are out. The average tenure of quoted company chief executives is now little more than three years and still falling. It is therefore no wonder that some have demanded huge salaries and stock options, and multi-year contracts that have to be paid out on termination, even if the executive is sacked for failing to deliver.

Looking at the different needs and expectations of the stakeholder groups allows an insight into some of the potential causes of reputational risk.

a)   Shareholders/owners

As a result of the UK government's encouragement of greater shareholder democracy, the number of private shareholders has risen significantly over the last two decades. Despite this success, the great majority of shares are still held by institutions (eg insurance companies, banks, pension funds, investment trusts) on behalf of their customers, clients or members, as well as on their own account.

In theory, all shareholders make an investment in a company to provide a combination of dividend income and capital growth, that makes up what is described as 'shareholder value'. In order to spread their risk they may invest in a number of companies, perhaps in a variety of industries, so as to produce a balanced portfolio.

As shareholders have acquired a financial interest in the future performance of the company, they would reasonably expect that the management, employed on their behalf to run the company, be competent, trustworthy and prudent with its finances, have a track record of delivery, and have a convincing strategy to deliver acceptable returns in the future.

The purpose of companies

The purpose of companies has moved historically from that of reducing risk for shareholders to that of maximising returns for shareholders. Of course, there has always been a tension between long-term shareholder return, such as is in theory argued for by the structure of our pension fund industry, and demands for short-term (ie annual or half-yearly) shareholder return, as is pushed for by our stock exchange system, and indeed the even shorter-term (sometimes overnight, or even hourly) shareholder return as is dreamt of and worked for by fund managers.

In purely legal terms, many companies particularly in the USA, feel that they would be on thin ice if they attempted to reinterpret the law (as companies such as BP are doing) to maximising returns over the long term, by paying more than minimum attention to stakeholders other than shareholders. As Milton Friedman memorably put it: 'Businessmen who believe that business has a "social conscience" and take seriously its responsibilities for providing employment, eliminating discrimination, avoiding pollution and whatever else may be the catchwords of the contemporary crop of reformers ..are...preaching pure and unadulterated socialism.'

That may be the reason why Professor Peter Drucker, who is often called the 'father of management' because of the extent of his influence in shaping management theory, recently said that most companies will not survive more than 25 years in the way they are constituted and run at present.

Professor Prabhu Guptara
Director, Executive & Organisational Development,
Wolfsberg Executive Development Centre (Switzerland)

In the past shareholders in quoted companies have usually been more passive than active, but now they are tending to be far more vociferous. These days AGMs can be quite stormy affairs, often agitated by disgruntled customers and other interest groups who might well have purchased a few shares just so they could confront the directors in a public meeting. Institutional shareholders too are beginning to flex their muscles, and have been taking a more direct role in looking to influence the management of companies in which they invest (eg on such issues as corporate governance or executive pay). This trend however is not as pronounced as one might expect, since many institutions still regard their prime duty to be protecting their own or their clients' financial interests, so they may sell the company's shares, rather than remain with a company until results improve.

A major influence on reputational risk was the growing power of the investment analysts in the bull market of the 1980s and 90s. However, significant concern over their independence and integrity (particularly in the US markets during the dotcom boom) has challenged their role and the way that they operate in the future. Nevertheless, they continue to serve an important function in tracking and analysing company and industry-wide performance, then advising investors to buy, sell or hold.

Those deemed to have expert knowledge of a sector can have huge influence. A negative report from a leading analyst (or worse, a rating agency like Standard & Poors or Moody) can severely damage a management's credibility. For this reason companies try to manage these relationships with great care. For their own part, the analysts often come in for the criticism that they encourage short termism and the churning of shares.

b)   Employees

Like a company's customers, its employees are all unique, have a complex set of needs, and a range of expectations of the company. Many companies would certainly benefit from directing a small proportion of the resources they currently spend on customer research to understanding their employees better. Undoubtedly the best companies do it as a matter of course, through continuous dialogue or by regular employee satisfaction surveys.

Need to understand employees' needs

It is a cliché, but employees are the lifeblood of a company, possess its core intellectual capital, and are the main interface with customers. It is strange therefore that a recent UK government report indicated that, in 80% of workplaces, there is a significant gap between what management knows to be good employment practice and the policies actually in place. It went on to say that this was having a corrosive effect on the employment relationship and generating mistrust in the workplace.

Obviously, fair reward and a safe working environment are a given in most societies (though not always a certainty in some businesses, particularly in less developed parts of the world). Beyond these, there may also be an expectation of greater involvement in decision making at all levels, more diversity to reflect society as a whole, longer holidays and more flexible working arrangements, career development opportunities, training, a wider range of non-statutory, non-pay benefits, etc. The current buzz phrase is work/life balance.

No-one these days can realistically expect a job for life, but many employees want the opportunity for continuous learning, at the very least, to make themselves more employable in the future. However, the often used management mantra that 'employees are in charge of their own careers' is usually a lame excuse for the abdication of a company's responsibility for the training and development of its employees.

Employee surveys/encouraging employee engagement

Employee engagement can be assessed in a number of ways, from focus groups to team briefings. However, it is employee surveys which offer the most objective means of measuring the true levels of employee engagement, particularly in large organisations. Many organisations will run some kind of employee satisfaction or opinion survey. However, commonly, these surveys are done in a way which renders the results close to useless.

What typically goes wrong:

Subjectivity: The problem with employee opinion and attitude surveys is that they are exactly that; measures of people's attitudes and opinions, not the true extent to which their psychological needs are being met on a sustained basis. Consequently, results are greatly influenced by how employees are feeling at the time they complete the survey. If they've just been given a bonus, scores soar. If they've just been turned down for promotion, scores plummet. These kinds of results will be of little use if the organisation wants to ascertain the true levels of employee engagement, the corresponding reputational risk and where to target improvements. What is more, the outputs of attitude and satisfaction surveys are often vague and clichéd. For example, it is hard to find a survey which does not indicate that pay, team-working and communication are problems.

Complexity: Often surveys attempt to measure a wide range of different organisational variables, not all of which are critical to employee engagement. As a consequence, the questionnaires can be extremely long – putting people off and reducing response rates, and complex – making data hard to interpret and therefore act on.

What you should do?

Keep it simple: There are a limited number of clearly definable factors which drive employee engagement. Focusing on these and avoiding 'nice to have' questions reduces complexity and questionnaire length, increases response rates and makes the results more useful.

Make it 'user-friendly': Plain English, short questionnaires, and a variety of delivery mechanisms (paper and pencil, intranet, internet) all lead to greater response rates.

Measure people's direct experience: ask questions about employees' personal experiences, not their opinions. For example, ask 'are you clear on what the goals of your business unit are?' rather than 'are the goals of the business unit communicated to your team effectively?. It is difficult to generate useful results from suppositions about the behaviours, attitudes and the feelings of others. Asking unambiguous questions about people's individual experiences helps reduce psychological biases due to fluctuations in mood and attitude.

Track improvements: Specify clearly what needs to improve and then help people measure their progress. Simple numerical indicators of performance direct attention to where it matters.

Benchmark: Allow comparisons, inside and outside the organisation. Benchmarking performance drives the achievement of increasingly high standards.

Measure the links to business results: The relationship between results on employee engagement surveys and business results such as profitability, customer satisfaction and sales should be examined using regression analysis. For example Kaisen research in a major UK retailer showed that a 1% increase in survey results was linked with a 10% increase in store sales per square foot.

Kaisen Consulting Ltd, 2004

Carry employees through major change

Without doubt the highest profile employee issues tend to concern major change programmes – re-engineering, transformation, outsourcing, new systems or methods of working. Too often these fail, irrespective of their merits, due to management not carrying their employees with them at every stage, and not convincing everyone of the necessity to change.

Bungled change programmes can be exceptionally damaging.

Today there is also a growing appreciation of stress at work. Whether or not the workplace is more stressful now than it has ever been is not the point. As far as reputational risk is concerned the issue is that employees are aware of the problem and expect there to be management policies in place to deal with it. If they are to protect their reputation, companies need to foster their relationship with their employees.

As Bruce Nixon, an acute observer of corporate behaviour, stated in *Global Forces*:

'Employers should care about disloyalty, low productivity, stress and absenteeism, as they end up being a massive cost to companies. The company's reputation starts to suffer.' He then goes on to describe how the bad news about the state of affairs within a company can spread rapidly from inside the company to the public at large.

BA flights disruption, July 2003

BA announced that the direct cost of the significant disruption to its flights, following staff walkouts over an attempt to introduce an electronic clocking-in system at Heathrow in July 2003, was more than £30m.

But the true cost of the reputational damage to BA, which resulted from this incident, could be much more in terms of additional costs over the coming years. The main areas of impact are likely to be in the areas of lost sales, and increased advertising and brand building spend, as the company seeks to rebuild its reputation for reliability and service (which had only recently been rebuilt), which was so publicly damaged following the staff walkout.

BA suffered further damage to its already battered reputation in the summer of 2004, with yet more flight cancellations and disruptions to services, reportedly as a result of having too few check-in staff available to handle customers during the peak holiday season and a shortage of spare parts for its aircraft undergoing routine maintenance. Staff unions claimed that both causes were the result of excessive cost cutting by management to improve financial performance. If true, this focus on shareholders would appear to have adversely impacted other stakeholders, specifically its customers and employees.

Change management: a cause of reputational risk in its own right

Research by the London Business School has shown that 75% of significant change efforts fail.

For CEOs, the success or failure of a major change initiative can be make or break. There are big rewards for turning companies round or successfully reorganising the business to deliver greater shareholder value. However, when change is poorly executed there are serious penalties. Projects fail to deliver on time or on budget, and when big promises made to the city or the media are not realised this can spell the beginning of the end for top executives. Probably the most significant impact of the failure to manage the people aspects of change is the impact on employee motivation and commitment. If staff turnover increases, the much-prized label of 'employer of choice' can be quickly lost and high profile staff disputes can rapidly take millions off a company's share price.

The reason why change fails is often that too much emphasis is placed upon project management methodologies, and the introduction of new technologies, without the systematic management of the people element. Whilst the practitioners in these areas will readily recognise the need to attend to the people aspects of change, to ensure that things move as quickly as possible, and new working practices are accepted readily, there is very little understanding on their part just how to do it, and even less understanding of how to do it systematically.

Kaisen Consulting Ltd, 2004

> " Our people must understand that, even in the most remote corner of the world a small incident can have massive repercussions. So if you think you are unimportant when it comes to Unilever's reputation – you are not. Everyone is important. "

Antony Burgmans, Joint-Chairman, Unilever

The importance of employees as stakeholders

Richard Smith, of Croner Consulting has said, 'Employees are a business's most important stakeholder group, and good employee relations are vital to the success and longevity of the business. However this is an area which is often neglected over keeping shareholders happy and attracting new investors.'

He recommends these practical measures to improve employee relations.

- Open channels of communication with employees through intranet, newsletter or regular meetings.
- Where practical, allow employees to participate in the decision-making process, for example through a vote.
- Inform employees of important decisions before they become known outside the company.
- Ask for employees' opinions and feedback.
- Set up a system where employees can appeal or complain against a decision and always address the matter with a suitable explanation or alternative.
- Listen to employees. Collectively, they can disrupt, or even bring to a halt, business activity if they feel they have been unfairly treated.

AMED News, Oct/Nov 2003

---

c) Customers

The vast majority of companies would claim to be 'customer focused'. They may well be driven by their responsibilities to shareholders, but they have to devote much of their resources to satisfying their customers. If they did not adopt this approach they would not stay in business for long in a climate where customers are better informed, less tolerant, and need little encouragement to complain, sue or take their business elsewhere.

Customers are looking for a subjective blend of quality, price and service: purchasing triggers are complex and can be hugely influenced by brand and reputation. When one looks at some of the highest profile losses of reputation in recent years they reveal certain basic customer expectations that were not satisfied.

◆ Safety – When demonstrable (Firestone tyres, Railtrack), or just merely suspected (GM foods).
◆ Fitness for Purpose – Pensions mis-selling.
◆ Transparency – Commission disclosure in financial services.
◆ Delivery of Promises – Mortgage endowments, guaranteed annuities, BA flights disruption summer 2003, Hoover's free airline tickets with every vacuum cleaner.

The last three bullet points help explain why the reputation of the UK life insurance industry has never been lower and may take years to recover. It was an industry obsessed with short-term sales rather than long-term customer satisfaction, so reputational damage has become systemic.

Even Coca Cola can get it wrong: the case of 'pure' Sidcup tap water

Despite the earlier quote from the CEO of Coca Cola, they too can get it wrong.

In 2003 Coca Cola launched the Dasani brand of bottled water in the UK with a major fanfare of advertising, placing the promotional emphasis on the product's 'purity'. However, when journalists asked questions about the source of the water, things quickly began to unravel.

◆ The source turned out to be the public mains supply in the south-east London suburb of Sidcup, (not previously known as a source of special note).

◆ Coca Cola filtered the water to remove the chlorine and other chemicals that it contained, before introducing its own additives to the filtered water to improve the taste – the promotional concept of 'purity' therefore took something of a knock.

◆ On scientific examination, the bottled water allegedly was found to contain minute traces of potentially harmful chemicals in greater quantities than in the initial tap water– creating media-based public health concerns (whether justified or not).

◆ The price being charged for the bottled water was around 95p per half litre, compared to the original cost of the tap water measured in fractions of a penny per litre – giving the impression of gross over-charging.

Trust in the product disappeared within weeks and the brand was withdrawn in the UK at a cost of millions of pounds.

Fortunately for Coca Cola as a corporation, there does not appear to have been any significant cross-over reputational damage to the company as a whole.

The lessons that emerge from this case study would appear to be.

◆ Customers react very strongly to any perception of being sold a 'false promise', or being misled or over-charged.

◆ Coca Cola, as a firm, were brave enough to kill the problem quickly, no matter the expense, thereby largely limiting damage to the Dasani brand itself, before it could significantly contaminate the corporate reputation.

Some writers suggest that customer expectations are also increasingly dependent on the means by which products are provided. They cite the successful impact of campaigns against sports equipment manufacturers, oil companies, clothing importers, supermarkets and many others who may be perceived to have condoned unethical practices elsewhere in the supply chain. As Bruce Nixon observed, 'It seems that ethical issues are important to many people, important enough to affect their purchasing and investment decisions.' Moreover, those with the most purchasing power are often the most likely to be first to vote with their feet and take their business elsewhere.

Companies may understand a lot about their customers as purchasers of products but, in this day and age, they may need to learn more about them as members of society.

d) Business partners and key suppliers

A company's relationship with its business partners (eg agents, outsourcing and other suppliers, joint venture partners, contractors) is two way. The parties should be working to aligned, or at least compatible, objectives, standards and values, or reputations on both sides may be put at risk. If something goes wrong with the end proposition, it is no use explaining to the customer that it was someone else's fault. The customer will expect the company to have managed its partnership relationships properly. This needs to be ensured not merely through the original written agreements and contracts, but through continuous dialogue, training, monitoring and audit.

When things go wrong it is *not* someone else's fault

With the current fashion for the deconstruction of value chains, (that is businesses concentrating on their own core areas of expertise and outsourcing the rest) the need to manage partner relationships effectively, and the link to the company's own reputational risk, can only become more important.

e) Government/ regulators

> America is ushering in a responsibility era, a culture regaining a sense of personal responsibility, and this new culture must include a renewed sense of corporate responsibility. Business relationships, like all human relationships, are built on a foundation of integrity and trust.

President George W. Bush

The government has a range of expectations of a company's behaviour.

◆ It will look for profitable enterprises that generate wealth, jobs and tax revenues.

◆ It will require 'responsible behaviour' in terms of:
  ● protection of the environment;
  ● good work practices;
  ● competitive and efficient markets;
  ● consumer and public protection in general; and
  ● compliance with all relevant regulations and law.

◆ There may also be expectations associated with the protection of national interests, whether in terms of security/defence or in other areas such as arts and culture, or scientific research.

Some of these expectations will be explicitly laid down in law, others may be through types of 'regulation', whether through a formal regulatory structure (eg OFGAS, OFGEM, OFWAT, FSA, the Competition Commission), through market or professional body 'self regulation' (the Stock Exchange, Professional Institutes) or through forms of 'best practice' instructions or guidance.

Increasingly, Government thinking is influenced by significant events such as disasters or major frauds, or by significant swings in public opinion, either evidenced by media campaigns, or via the lobbying of NGOs. This has tended, over recent years, to emphasise 'customer protection' at what might be seen by some as the expense of the best interests of business in general.

Over the long term, there seem to be distinct cycles of government intervention via regulation. The pendulum has swung from the de-regulation of the 1980s–1990s to an increasingly rules-based regime. A swing back is inevitable in due course, but for the time being companies will have to meet increasingly high levels of government or regulatory expectations (compliance) across many different aspects of their operations.

f) The general public, media and NGOs

Members of the public in general will have expectations regarding how a company should behave. They can broadly be divided into:

◆ the local community and media;
◆ the general public and national or international media; and
◆ special interest groups.

The local community has an immediate and obvious interest in any company that operates in its midst. There will be expectations about it bringing employment and economic benefits to the area, while at the same time maintaining a safe and healthy environment. There may also be calls for the company to have an active community investment programme: sponsorship, working with schools, sharing sports facilities, involvement with local charities, fund raising events, etc. Since many companies do not have structured programmes for this kind of activity, clearly not everyone considers it to be enlightened self interest, or at best it is worthy of only ad hoc interest, as events arise. Perhaps more companies would participate if they brought reputational risk into the equation.

The media are key opinion leaders, locally and nationally. Businesses should identify the issues that might affect their reputation and try to influence these opinion formers. Many companies are hesitant about dealing with the media, and only begin to have a proper dialogue with them when a problem has arisen. By then it may be too late. Negative sentiment is usually the reward for a neglected relationship. At the other end of the scale are those organisations who believe in the triumph of PR over substance. This may be fine for a short period, but as soon as promises are not delivered, or partial truths discovered for what they are, the company's reputation can be destroyed.

Neglect of the media results in negative sentiment

The other influencers of public opinion that may have a substantial impact on a company's reputation are the special interest groups. There are literally thousands of these in the UK, and hundreds of thousands worldwide. They range from a handful of people focused on a specific local issue, to giants like Greenpeace, Friends of the Earth and Amnesty International with tens of thousands of members and a global reach. They engage in lobbying, publicity, legal action and, in some cases, direct action.

The larger of these special interest groups are often referred to as Non-Governmental Organisations (NGOs), such is their influence. They have now become part of the accepted political process, with governments consulting them as representatives of the views of the general public. In turn, NGOs have attracted criticism for wielding power without accountability.

NGOs are now part of the political process

41

The ability of special interest groups to mobilise interest on an issue has increased by an order of magnitude since the advent of the internet. It is possible for a small group (or just an individual) to generate significant publicity for their 'specific issue' through the use of the internet and website technology, by attracting the interest of 'activists looking for a cause', which can be out of all proportion to the significance of the issue itself. Thus, even small specific interest groups need to be taken notice of and monitored by companies who might be impacted by their activities.

Pressure for corporate social responsibility

    It is no longer enough to focus on internal objectives alone: outside-in thinking – thinking on a much wider scale about an organisation's relationship with society – is an essential prerequisite for achieving the tacit acceptance of society to continue to operate.

Judy Larkin, Think Outside–In, International Risk Management, Oct 1997

    NGOs still put pressure on governments and inter-governmental bodies, but during the 1990s the aim has shifted towards business.

Investing in Social Responsibility, Association of British Insurers, 2000

    Public companies in the US and the UK, still recovering from the shock dealt to their systems by the implementation of corporate governance processes, now found themselves facing a new dilemma – the assault to their reputation and share price as a result of sustained publicity campaigns against them.

Roger Cowe, No Scruples

Corporate strategy and corporate communications/PR

As you may infer from the authors' experience in introducing the stakeholder model, strategic planning has considerable potential to influence the propensity for reputational risk. As reputational risk arises from a mismatch between what a company does and the reasonable expectations of its stakeholders, there should be an effort made to ensure that the company's plans and those expectations are aligned as far as is practical, or at least not incompatible. Of course, one should not slavishly follow the other; hopefully we are talking about maintaining an adult-to-adult relationship between the parties. However, it is evident that a thorough analysis and understanding of the current and potential stakeholders' expectations should form a core element of the strategic planning process. This is essentially what some commentators have described as 'outside-in thinking'. It may seem obvious, but such an approach is rarely, if ever, mentioned in management textbooks.

The mirror image of allowing stakeholders to influence the company, is the company's opportunity to foster the stakeholder relationship and, where possible, 'manage expectations'.

Many cases of reputational damage are incremental, the result of the neglect of a particular stakeholder relationship, or perhaps a number of small incidents building up and gradually undermining the external perception of the company.

The prevention of these circumstances is normally the province of the corporate communications, or PR, function.

What the public thinks

In one US survey, members of the public were asked to identify the most important 'values' for businesses to uphold. The results, in order of perceived importance, were as follows:

1. providing quality products and services;

2. having ethical business practices;

3. protecting the environment;

4. contributing to the local environment;

5. sharing profits with employees;

6. providing a good return to investors.

The survey indicated that while the public believe companies generally do a good job in providing quality products and a good investor return, they believe they fall short in the other categories.

Risk Management Reports, Vol 26 No 10, Oct 1999

Professionals in this area need to be closely attuned to, and monitor, the various stakeholder groups; ensuring that key stakeholder relationships are maintained, and that stakeholder expectations do not become out of line with what the company does, or plans to do. A golden rule for successful PR is that there should be 'no surprises'.

Even the most highly regarded companies can get it wrong if they underestimate the weight of public opinion. Taking the position 'we the company know best' can lead to a humiliating climb-down, should the stakeholders become sufficiently concerned to decide to exercise their powers. When the Bank of Scotland attempted to enter a joint venture with a US

The golden rule of PR is 'no surprises'

Gradually emerging issues

 An emerging issue or trend, which at first sight may not appear to be significant, could have the potential to place your organisation in a vulnerable position.

Judy Larkin, Think Outside–In, International Risk Management, Oct 1997

financial services company that was owned by a person with known extreme views on gender, sexuality and race, the bank's stakeholders were alarmed and many customers and investors threatened to withdraw their business. The bank responded by announcing: 'there's a reputational risk to almost every area we do business, such as some building projects. It is a question of trying to behave responsibly in a way that society as a whole accepts. Most new initiatives upset some special interest groups. It would be almost impossible if you tried to please everyone.'

However, soon afterwards, the bank felt obliged to abandon its plans, admitting an error of judgement and apologising to its stakeholders.

There is much that a proactive corporate communications team can do in terms of reputational risk management. However, no reputation can be maintained indefinitely without substance. Whatever is said must be as true and frank as possible, within the bounds of commercial confidentiality. 'Spin', manipulating the media, or being economical with the truth, is always counterproductive in the long run. Once an organisation, single executive or executive team has been caught out, no one will trust them again for a long time, even if they are telling the truth – as political parties have found to their cost.

'Spin' is counter-productive in the long term

The problems of not meeting expectations

Elsewhere in this book we have used Unilever as an example of good practice of a multinational company managing its reputation and conducting itself ethically and responsibly, but even the best can sometimes fail to meet expectations, with significant consequences.

Even though Unilever continued to meet its challenging earnings targets, investors and analysts felt let down by this failure to meet expectations, and marked the stock down in consequence.

❝❝ The consumer goods giant's shares have plunged 17.5 per cent since January, ranking them among the worst performers in the FTSE 100. The management would like to blame the late Dr Atkins whose diet fad has cost Unilever's Slimfast about a third of its sales, but the fault lies closer to home. Twice this year the company has downgraded expectations of its leading brand growth, from 5-6pc to 4pc, and then last week to 'below 3pc'. ❞❞

Daily Telegraph Questor Column, 30 October 2003

Conclusion

We hope that, by this stage, we have demonstrated that an appreciation of the stakeholder model is of key importance when approaching the management of reputational risk. The concept is by no means new, and merely echoes the early days of company incorporation, when it was generally accepted that companies had a wider societal purpose, and were not solely there to enrich their shareholders.

'Focus' may mean increased reputational risk

If your chief executive announces, 'I have decided that the company is going to be focused (on profit, customers, shareholder value, or whatever)', stop and think.

It is good that the company now has leadership and strategic direction, but consider what other stakeholder interests are being sidelined. The word 'focus' almost always carries with it an increase in reputational risk which needs to be recognised and managed.

Obviously, shareholders' needs and expectations must have a significant influence over the company's activities, but the current obsession with their short-term, rather than longer-term, needs is a relatively recent phenomenon. Shareholder focused short termism may satisfy 'some of the people for some of the time', but it undoubtedly increases the threat of reputational risks, particularly in relation to other stakeholders, and is quite likely to not even be in the shareholders' long-term interests.

A company wishing to manage its reputational risk needs to understand the range of its stakeholders' expectations, and seek to achieve alignment between these expectations and what the company plans to do.

The need to look at oneself from the perspective and expectations of others is not new. One Sunday morning in church over two hundred years ago, the Scottish poet

Bad business

66 I think short-term business is bad business. But you do have to have survived to have a long-term business. All my working life we knew that business depended on people. People mattered. Things have gone badly wrong… people are not motivated because everything is now share price orientated. 99

Sir John Harvey Jones, The Guardian, 16 August 2003

Robert Burns sat behind a lady wearing an expensive hat. Unfortunately for the lady's reputation, closer inspection of her hat revealed that a louse (a blood sucking parasitic insect) had taken up residence therein. This inspired Burns to write these immortal lines, in his southern Scottish dialect:

O wad some pow'r the giftie gie us
To see oursels as others see us!
It wad frae mony a blunder free us

Reputation does not depend on what we think of ourselves. What really matters is what the outside world perceives and believes.

Chapter 3:

Managing corporate performance and behaviour

On completing this chapter you will have begun to build an understanding as to why:

- ◆ in most companies management control processes tend to be focused on shareholder-driven financial and performance measures;
- ◆ much reputational risk arises from other stakeholder expectations, which may be behavioural in nature;
- ◆ in this context, ethical best practice, the adoption of optimum standards of corporate behaviour and citizenship, begins to make far greater sense;
- ◆ like other management requirements, desirable behaviour needs to be defined, codified, taught and monitored;
- ◆ desirable behaviour needs to be linked to individuals' personal performance assessments.

In the first two chapters of this book, we looked at the nature of, and some of the challenges faced in managing, reputational risk in general and the issues presented by the range of differing stakeholder expectations that need to be taken into account. In this third chapter, we explore the issues surrounding the need to manage corporate and employee behaviours, as well as the performance of a company, if reputational risk is to be dealt with effectively. We also demonstrate why commitment to a range of non-revenue generating 'corporate good citizenship' activities can actually be good for business when reputational risk is factored into the equation.

Managing performance

To repeat the definition of reputational risk proposed earlier:

Reputational risk = **Failure to meet stakeholders' reasonable expectations of an organisation's performance *and* behaviour.**

Most companies have highly developed processes and procedures to monitor and manage company performance in financial terms because:

♦ they are required to maintain accurate and up to date financial records by law;

♦ shareholders and the investment markets expect regular (and ever more detailed) information on the financial performance of companies;

♦ financial performance is, relatively, much easier to measure than other performance factors, because of the common units of measurement which can be attached to transactions, assets, liabilities, costs, etc, the majority of which are already recorded in the financial records as a normal part of day-to-day record keeping.

As a result, financial performance has, over the latter part of the 20th century, become the overriding measure and driver for a company and its management, in some companies to the exclusion of nearly all other performance measures. With the increasing focus on the short term by the investment markets, this has led to pressure for continually improving financial performance (eg profit, growth) ratcheting up quarter after quarter. As a result, some commentators, including the authors, believe that management have often made decisions that, while beneficial in terms of short-term financial reporting, are actually damaging to the long-term interests of the company. Such actions include 'inappropriate' acquisitions, cost cutting that removes core intellectual capital from the organisation, and failure to 'invest for the future' (eg in training, R+D, new products, strategic thinking).

Financial performance has become the overriding driver in most organisations

Excessive focus on short-term financial performance can lead to poor performance (and therefore a failure to meet stakeholder expectations) in other areas, either through 'neglect', or where financial performance drivers conflict with the performance drivers for the other area. Our view of relative stakeholder interest in a range of company performance areas is given in the table below for a 'typical' company:

Relative importance of performance areas to the different stakeholders

AREA / STAKE HOLDER	Financial performance	Product/ service quality	Legal compliance	Social responsibility (including environmental)	Fairness/ honesty
Shareholders/ owners	5	3	3	1	1
Customers	3	5	3	2	4
Employees	3	3	4	2	5
Suppliers/ partners	2	3	3	1	5
Government/ regulators	2	3	5	4	5
Public/NGOs	2	2	5	5	5

5 = of highest importance to the stakeholders

3 = of reasonable importance to the stakeholders

1 = of some importance, but less than other areas

It is suggested therefore that, while of some interest to all stakeholders, the overall financial performance of a company is only of significant interest (a score of 4-5) to shareholders/owners, while the primary interests of all other stakeholder groups lie in other areas of company performance.

The non-financial performance areas are harder to measure, but are becoming increasingly important to companies, with growing involvement by government and regulators; influence of pressure groups; and a 'compensation culture', where companies may be taken to court by any aggrieved party that considers they have been damaged or unfairly treated. As a result, stakeholders will increasingly expect companies to demonstrate how they are performing across a wide range of non-financial areas, and companies will need processes and measures with which to manage, monitor and report on this performance. Areas where increased reporting on non-financial performance is becoming more onerous include: various sets of rules and guidance on internal controls and risk management and reporting thereon; compliance with legislation and regulation; and environmental impacts. Additional requirements are likely to develop over time.

One means of managing a company on a mixture of financial and non-financial measures is the balanced scorecard.

The balanced scorecard

Since the advent of the computer there has been no shortage of internal data available to businesses. In fact, in many companies, there is so much data available that the manager's job is probably more driven by numbers than ever. The problem is that, in order to manage a company effectively, data must provide relevant information. In other words, management should be concentrating on those selected measures that best show how the company is performing.

That doyen of management writers, Peter Drucker, has long maintained that business performance cannot be measured by financial data alone. Other metrics, such as customer satisfaction, quality, and innovation may reveal a company's condition and prospects more closely than historic accounting data. In 1992 Norton and Kaplan at Harvard Business School published radical ideas to help address this perceived corporate over-emphasis on financial and internal measurement. They proposed a technique that has come to be known as the balanced scorecard.

In the balanced scorecard, goals, predictive measures and actual outcomes are developed to provide a 'balanced' set of views of company performance, taking into consideration both financial and non-financial, and internal and external information and measurements. The approach is far more holistic than that formerly adopted. In the original Harvard version the four 'views' were:

◆ **financial perspective** (How do we look to the shareholders?) eg ROC, profit, cash flow;

◆ **customer perspective** (How do customers see us?) eg Market Share, Complaints, Media Profile;

◆ **internal business perspective** (What must we excel at?) eg quality, key project milestones, service function, service levels;

◆ **innovation and learning** (Can we continue to improve and create value?) eg employee surveys, competency levels.

Companies have expanded the concept further and the 'views' may be adapted to include a wider range of stakeholder needs, eg legal compliance, environmental performance.

The balanced scorecard in practice

Through use of the balanced scorecard, the UK Ministry of Defence (MOD) has integrated risk management into its performance management regime so that, every time the Defence Management Board considers performance, it considers risk too. This means that the Department has, at board-level and each strategic business unit-level, a regular assessment of the key risks that are being managed across the organisation and the impact they are likely to have on performance across the span of its objectives.

The Defence Balanced Scorecard provides a natural framework for identifying and managing risk and a tool that assists the Department in defining its appetite boundaries. The Scorecard's key performance indicators define a set of strategic and operational metrics, which measure performance against the Department's objectives and goals. Through factoring Department-wide risks into performance measurement, and recognising that there are operational limits beyond which corrective actions are required in order to remain within the path defined by the strategy, the Scorecard enables key risk indicators (KRIs) to be defined, and risk appetite boundaries to be drawn through key performance indicators (KPIs).

Group Captain Ian MacEachern OBE, RAF
UK Ministry of Defence

Some management teams may strongly resist the introduction of balanced scorecards, often criticising them as irrelevant bureaucracy. In our experience this may be due to one of two reasons. First, the scorecard may be made up of a hotchpotch of measures, that might well be interesting in their own right, but fail to come together to define a coherent strategic direction. Secondly, and more likely, managers' performance-related rewards are not aligned with the range of scorecard measures. It is still the norm in many companies for individuals to be primarily incentivised according to financial performance criteria alone.

Incentivisation is often linked only to financial performance

The risk of 'inappropriate incentives'

If staff incentives are not fully aligned and coherent with the organisation's range of strategic objectives, stakeholders' expectations, policies and culture, staff may be encouraged to behave or perform in a manner that is not in the overall best interests of the organisation. Examples could include the following.

51

◆ Salesmen rewarded solely on 'volume' may be encouraged to sell goods or services at less than cost, or that are inappropriate to the customer's needs (eg the sale of some financial services products).

◆ Managers driven by cost-cutting objectives may be encouraged to 'cut too deep', damaging employee morale and customer service quality, and losing important skills and experience which could have a detrimental impact on the organisation's future performance.

Reputation is as important for other organisations as it is for companies

Charities

  ❝❝ Reputation is an important component of any modern company, but it is absolutely vital to a charity. Whilst some fund raising activities might produce short-term revenues (eg pavement 'chuggers', that is paid fund raisers who accost and pressure sell to members of the public in the street) it remains to be seen if these tactics will create long-term damage to the reputation of the charities themselves, or the charity sector as a whole. ❞❞

Mark Evans, Continuity, Insurance and Risk Magazine

Political parties

There has always been a healthy suspicion of political parties but their current reputation in Europe and North America is as low as it has ever been. The root cause is that politicians have to make promises to be elected or stay in office, and these create expectations in the electorate. Of course, real government is never as simple as it may appear in a party manifesto and a gap between what politicians say and what they actually do is inevitable. The situation is made worse as the modern party has had to live with 24-hour media scrutiny constantly reminding it of its shortcomings.

As the journalist Jeremy Paxman pointed out in his perceptive book, The Political Animal: 'as the gap grew, so did the public distrust of politics and politicians'.

A further reason for the decline in the reputation of political parties is the impossible, and rather hypocritical, requirement encouraged by the media that anyone in public life must demonstrate a higher standard of personal morality than the people they represent. Of course it is unfair, but increasingly politicians are having to accept that it goes with the job.

Shell's overstated oil reserves

'Auditors at Shell warned that an internal bonus system might encourage reserve levels to be inflated two years before Shell said it had overstated its 'proven' barrels by 23%, the *Wall Street Journal* claims.'

Daily Telegraph news item, 16 July 2004

Shell will abolish 'discovery bonus'

Chairman hopes switch from exploration-fuelled perks will avoid temptation to overstate oil giant's assets

Crisis-hit Shell is scrapping a controversial scheme which links staff pay levels to the amount of oil and gas employees find. The news is the latest attempt by Shell to restore its reputation after its disastrous admission that it had exaggerated its 'proven' oil and gas reserves by 23% earlier this year.

The company is hoping a new bonus scheme, to be introduced in January, will encourage Shell's 90,000 employees to work for the good of the group, rather than Shell's individual business units.

Jeroen van der Veer, the [new] chairman of Shell's committee of managing directors said in an interview that the new bonus scheme would encourage staff to think 'enterprise first' rather than 'self first'. Mr van der Veer had been concerned about whether the balance between 'enterprise first' and 'self first' had moved too much to 'self first'. He added that ambition is good 'but ambition with disregard for peers or subordinates creates the wrong culture'.

Presently, all Shell staff are eligible for an annual bonus, which depends on company and individual performance. These criteria will be replaced by a group-wide 'one-size-fits-all bonus'.

Controversial bonuses for exploration and production staff, which were linked to oil reserve replacement, will also be axed under the plans. These bonuses were seen as wrongly providing staff with an incentive which could lead them to exaggerate reserve levels.

A Shell spokesman said: 'Multiple score cards will be replaced by single group score cards, focusing on execution of strategy, delivery of operational objectives and enterprise first. Enterprise first addresses the importance of group needs over the needs of individual operating units. We hope to have the new score cards in place for the calendar year 2005 bonus scheme.'

> William Claxton-Smith, director of UK equities at Insight which has a 1.1% stake said: 'We believe that it is important companies set appropriate targets for their staff. It appears that this oil replacement target acted as a perverse incentive.'
>
> *Extract from news article,* **Daily Telegraph**, *30 August 2004*

Managing behaviour

In addition to company performance, stakeholder expectations are also linked to company behaviour: not just the company as a corporate whole, but also the behaviour of individual employees or groups of employees. Behaviour is to do with how a company or individual acts in response to a specific situation, rather than 'performance' which is essentially a longer-term measure. Behaviour is also intrinsically linked to the culture of the organisation. So the challenge is for the company to firstly codify the culture or behavioural standards it expects to be in place, and then ensure that its employees, and the company as a whole, behave in a way that is consistent with them.

As noted earlier, the behaviour of a single individual or small group of employees can seriously damage the reputation of a company, whether it be inappropriate comments of a senior executive, the publicity resulting from an industrial tribunal case that discloses inappropriate behaviours, or the way the company as a whole treats its suppliers or customers.

Managing behaviour is different

Managing behaviour requires different competences from those of managing numbers. These include a range of what might be termed 'soft' skills: observation, mentoring, hands-on support and guidance, walking the talk, leading by positive example. People can be forced to act in a way that is inconsistent with their natural instincts or personal cultural norms through rigid controls, penalties for non-conformance, etc, but managing behaviour will always be more effective where the desired behaviour is consistent with the individual's personal beliefs of what is reasonable or correct.

Top down and bottom up

Controlling business behaviour can be approached from two directions – top down (corporate), or bottom up (individual).

- ◆ In the more prescriptive top-down approach, a company may establish principles and rules which should guide its business and lie alongside the strategies and plans. These may appear in a variety of forms such as policies for corporate culture and brand values, stakeholder charters, statements of business principles, and compliance rules.

◆ The bottom-up approach involves giving employees ethics training and other behavioural guidance, which they are expected to apply to situations as they arise.

In practice, there is not always a clear distinction between the two approaches and companies may do both. Some companies, particularly smaller ones, have little documented evidence for either. In small, owner-managed companies this lack can be made up for by the hands-on involvement of the owner demonstrating the required behaviours on a daily basis. In larger companies, any such lack can create a vacuum of uncertainty as to what is expected, allow significant inconsistency in the behaviours of staff to occur, or make it difficult for staff behaviours to be managed effectively.

Difficulties of control

Big companies have never been easy to control, but in recent years it has probably become even harder. Organisations get larger and more complex, hierarchies are de-layered, matrix management structures are established, authority is devolved and value chains disaggregated while, at the same time, the external environment and stakeholder expectations of the company continue to change. As a result, management's ability to maintain control over every aspect of corporate behaviour is potentially diminished even further. In many organisations the old, rigid command structures have gone, particularly in the private sector, and this is one of the frustrations of regulators. When they issue directives to companies they often find it strange that they are not implemented immediately.

Corporate self-delusion

In large companies, it is not at all uncommon for the chief executive, having specified codes of conduct or other non-financial performance standards for the company and its employees, to firmly believe that such policies are being complied with, when in fact they are not. The incorrect reporting can be the result of poor systems or processes trying to measure and manage relatively intangible elements of performance or, on occasion, management may simply be telling the chief executive what they want to hear, because they are unable to implement the required standards in practice.

The board's need to understand the business that they run

The Shell case, mentioned earlier, emphasises the point made in the Penrose Report into the collapse of Equitable Life Assurance in the UK – that it is not sufficient for a board of directors to merely accept information that is presented to them by the company executives or other experts. It is their duty to obtain a proper understanding of the issues being considered, and to question (and if necessary challenge) the information put before them. Where this relates to extremely complex and technical issues (such as in the Equitable Life case regarding the actuarial and legal implications of guaranteed annuity rates in contracts sold, or the appropriateness and accuracy of oil reserve calculation methodologies in the case of Shell) the board must dedicate sufficient time to acquire the necessary understanding of the issues before making decisions, otherwise incorrect decisions could be made that significantly damage the reputation or viability of the business.

Whilst the Penrose Report is not binding on UK companies in general, it is likely that the essence of its recommendations in this area will be incorporated into the UK's Combined Code on Corporate Governance at its next revision.

Does management receive appropriate training in how to handle the wide range of causes of reputational risk?

Management development and training has been slow to equip leaders to deal with the changed circumstances noted above. Professor Prabhu Guptara has observed that the traditional approach to management training does not equip executives with some of the competences really needed by today's companies. It may be excellent in developing executives with financial and selling skills, but it is very weak in producing executives able to deal effectively with the increasingly important, but less easily measured, intangible areas such as the management of: brand values, culture, ethics, human rights, environmental concerns, corporate governance or corporate affairs.

Decision making and reputational risk

The business psychologists, Kaisen Consulting, have studied the impact of decision making on reputational risk and suggested that developing a manager's problem solving ability could well be helpful in managing this risk. They told us:

" Look back through history and you'll find that most reputational disasters can be traced back to bad business decision making. The British Airways tailfin fiasco, the Ratner 'crap jewellery' saga and the demise of Equitable Life are just a few examples. For those working in marketing and PR, thinking about the reputation dimension will be a natural day-to-day activity. Why? Because through experience, they have learned to spontaneously attend to these factors when making decisions. Much like the salesperson naturally notices the response in the customer groups, the PR manager intuitively considers the implications of decisions on the business' reputation. However, commonly the people most responsible for the reputational catastrophes work in non PR-related functions. So the lesson is: if the organisation is serious about safeguarding against reputational risk, every manager in every function should be thinking about the reputation dimension as well as the customer, cost and competitor angles they may already be attending to.

So, how can organisations develop managers' thinking so that they are spontaneously considering reputational risk? Of course there are a multitude of different programmes available which claim to help managers make better decisions. They can learn 'finance for non-financial managers', 'strategic planning' and 'commercial decision making', all of which will give them a better understanding of those subject areas. However, the real problem is that managers need to change the way they think, not what they are thinking about. More specifically, they need to increase the breadth and depth of their schema (their experiential problem solving ability) in order to make effective decisions and avoid making errors of judgement. "

Kaisen Consulting Ltd, 2004

A treasurer's concern

❝❝ Successful money dealers tend to be young, highly competitive, alpha male types, preoccupied with making money for themselves. Some would have made great street traders. Senior management don't understand them. Very few of the dealers themselves are able to make the jump to management as they are required to look after more interests than just their own. As a result, there is almost a disconnect between the dealing room and the rest of the organisation. ❞❞

Corporate Treasurer, Financial Institution

Why a commitment to corporate social responsibility (good corporate citizenship) is an important element in protecting against reputational risk

These days, as previously suggested, stakeholder expectations are increasingly focused on how the company performs and behaves in relation to society or the environment, either just locally to its operations or in the wider world. A company's reputation can therefore be significantly damaged if these wider expectations are not met. Many of these expectations are commonly rolled up under the generalised term CSR (corporate social responsibility) which includes, amongst other things, ethical and behavioural standards, approaches to legal and regulatory compliance, environmental issues, and community involvement.

The difficulty that most companies face is in trying to understand the reputational risk associated with failing to meet stakeholder expectations in these areas, and thereby understanding how much resource it is worth allocating to improve the company's reputation, or protect it from reputational damage arising in these areas. Typical challenges might be.

◆ What quantum of damage could be caused to the reputation of the company by failing to actively engage with the local community in which it operates, eg not supporting or giving time or resources to local charities or schools?

◆ Will any failure to engage with the local community have an impact on its ability to recruit the best staff in the future or make changes to its business more difficult?

◆ What is the impact on the company's reputation if it deliberately acts in a way that is less than current environmental best practice, but still perfectly legal?

◆ What is the potential impact on the company of acting in a perfectly legal way with regard to its employees, suppliers, neighbours, etc, but where that approach damages the goodwill of these key stakeholders, or is viewed by other stakeholders (eg NGOs) as unacceptable?

The importance of corporate social responsibility to an organisation's reputation

> The environmental and social performance of companies can also have significant effect on intangible assets such as brand image and consumer goodwill, which are recognised as key to company reputation and trust.

Sustainability Reporting Guidelines 2002,
Global Reporting Initiative

> BP's good deeds are 'in our direct business interests, not acts of charity, but of what could be called enlightened self-interest... Performance is enhanced when a company is aligned with the interests of its consumers... The reputation of a company in the widest sense has a direct impact on its commercial fortunes.'

Sir John Browne, Chairman, BP

> In an interview with Joel Bakan, Milton Friedman, the world famous economist, argued the following: 'There is but one social responsibility for corporate executives: they must make as much money as possible for their shareholders. This is a moral imperative. Executives who choose social and environmental goals over profit — who try to act morally — are, in fact, immoral. .... (However) the executive who treats social and environmental values as a means to maximise shareholders wealth — not as ends in themselves — commits no wrong.'

quoted in **The Corporation**, *Joel Bakan*

As stated previously, it may be very difficult to accurately measure the potential reputational damage from not acting as a good corporate citizen. But, even without accurate measurement, most companies should be able to make an estimate of the impact on their business of a fundamental loss of trust in the company from the four stakeholder groups other than investors and customers.

- ◆ **Employees** – eg poor pay or working conditions, lack of recognition of non-financial needs (union representation, work-life balance).
- ◆ **Key suppliers and business partners** – eg bullying or overly hard price negotiations, slow payment, overly demanding quality standards.
- ◆ **Government and regulators**: government agencies (eg Inland Revenue, Customs & Excise, health and safety, environment, employment), local government (eg planning, rating, waste disposal, trading standards), regulators and professional and industry standards setters (eg FSA, Monopolies Commission, OFWAT, the Stock Exchange, Accounting Standards Board,

industry associations) – all such bodies can make life extremely difficult for a company if the company is believed to be non-compliant with their rules, codes or other formal expectations.

◆ **The general public**, especially the media and special interest groups (including NGOs) whether local, national or international – poor management, corporate greed or fraud, lack of respect for communities, the environment, Third World suppliers, current and potential customers, or the public in general.

It is worth re-emphasising that particular stakeholder expectations can sometimes be ignored in the short term, sometimes with relatively little immediate impact. However, we believe that if, in the longer term, the reasonable expectations of an important stakeholder group are not met, then the company can expect to face considerable difficulties and threats to its future success.

Increasing expectations of corporate governance

Pressures on corporations to establish and maintain high standards of internal governance are accelerating. As society witnesses the growing influence of corporations in driving economic, environmental, and social change, investors and other stakeholders expect the highest standards of ethics, transparency, sensitivity, and responsiveness from corporate executives and managers. Governance systems are increasingly expected to extend beyond their traditional focus on investors to address diverse stakeholders. The independence of board members, executive participation in external partnerships, compensation and incentive schemes, and integrity of auditors are under increasing scrutiny. Effective corporate governance depends on access to relevant, high-quality information that enables performance tracking and invites new forms of stakeholder engagement. The proliferation of corporate governance initiatives – the Cadbury Commission and the Turnbull Report in the UK, the King Report in South Africa, Brazil's innovative New Stock Exchange, the OECD's Guidelines for Multinational Enterprises and Corporate Governance Principles, and the World Bank's Corporate Governance Forum – attest to rising expectations for high standards of corporate behaviour.

Sustainability Reporting Guidelines 2002,
Global Reporting Initiative

Using conventional risk assessment techniques, it is possible to establish judgmental measures (High/ Medium/ Low) of impact and likelihood for all potential causes of damage. This may be a time consuming process the first time it is attempted, not least because of the huge range of potential causes of reputational damage in these areas. Consultants, such as the big insurance brokers, can be extremely helpful at this stage, as they can be objective and bring experience of how similar companies have addressed issues. Once established, such judgmental measures can provide positive guidance as to the relative importance of the risks faced, and therefore indicate to managers where it is important to focus resources in protecting the company's reputation.

In our opinion, most stakeholder groups' expectations of 'good corporate citizenship' will increase considerably over the coming years. As a result, companies will need to continually improve their level of performance in the relevant areas if they believe that it remains in their interest to meet these expectations.

Expectations of good corporate citizenship will increase

In addition to our contention that a company needs to look at its corporate citizenship behaviours in order to manage reputational risk, proposed changes to company reporting emphasise the need for directors of companies to assess and understand the less quantifiable risks and issues facing the company, including the range of expectations of their various stakeholders both now and in the future.

Other influences on company behaviour

In addition to potentially having to meet the increasing non-financial performance expectations of a range of different stakeholders, as discussed above, there are a range of other influences of company behaviour.

In a modern developed economy there are, typically, many external organisations or bodies that produce non-statutory codes of practice for behaviour, either for companies or individual employees. There is nothing new in this, the trade guilds and their modern day counterparts the professional institutes have been doing this for hundreds of years. Professional codes, like those of lawyers, doctors and accountants, tend to be compulsory, in that a person infringing the rules can be struck off. Industry or market codes, such as the Banking Code, are usually voluntary. Nevertheless, a company not formally subscribing to its industry code should be working to at least that standard of behaviour implied by the code, as this would be the minimum to satisfy public and other stakeholders' expectations.

The existence of external codes can give rise to considerable conflicts of interest for an employee should they find that company practice is at odds with the requirements of other codes.

Do companies need anything more to manage behaviour?

The study of ethics, essentially what constitutes right and wrong, has occupied some of the greatest minds over successive millennia. Unfortunately it can become very academic and a 'turn off' for many managers.

Proposals for additional reporting

The UK Government White Paper 'Modernising Company Law' (July 2002), and the subsequent consultation paper issued by the Operating and Financial Review Working Group (July 2003), made proposals to considerably increase the obligations on directors to produce a more meaningful Operating and Financial Review (OFR) in the company's Report and Accounts. (Though the requirement for a structured OFR was subsequently dropped, the same essential requirements are expected to be contained in new EU company reporting regulations.)

'The high level objective (of the OFR) is to enable users to assess the strategies adopted by the business and the potential for successfully achieving them.'

As a result, the proposals included an obligation on directors, when reporting, to:

◆ take into account both the current and future expectations of a wide range of stakeholders;

◆ assess the significance of the wider issues identified in the Company Law Review such as environmental, community, social or ethical considerations;

◆ include such matters as are material to the business, judged in the context of the risks, opportunities and threats facing the business, including an assessment of non-financial issues such as environmental, ethical or reputational risk;

◆ consider the future impact of issues, not just their quantifiable impact today;

◆ include material issues even if they are unquantifiable.

And produce 'a description of the principal risks and uncertainties facing the business ...'

'Such matters will need to be assessed in the context of the risks, opportunities and threats facing the business, including an assessment of non-financial issues that can have significant consequences for future performance and value ... A particularly important issue related to risk is the **reputation of the business**. This is inextricably linked to the licence to operate and is a critical value driver. Reputation, and thus competitive advantage, may be won or lost through the ability to deliver consistently against explicit or implicit promises made to investors and other key stakeholders, including customers, suppliers and employees.'

The Operating and Financial Review
Practical Guidance for Directors, May 2004

As far as reputational risk is concerned, the niceties of the philosophical arguments surrounding ethics are largely irrelevant. Companies need to determine what is deemed acceptable behaviour, at a practical level, in the societies in which they operate, as that should represent what the majority of stakeholders care about, and therefore what they expect from companies. In most societies they would expect a company to display honesty, fairness, integrity, openness, legality and distributive justice. In other words, they want 'good corporate citizenship'.

Need to define 'acceptable behaviour'

For the remainder of this book we will use the term **ethical best practice** to mean optimum standards of good corporate behaviour and citizenship.

Are business schools teaching self-destruction?

The late Professor Sumantra Ghoshal of London Business School blamed the increase in corporate scandals on the teaching of business academics over the last three decades. He felt that they had taught managers to create new ways of inflating share prices, paying themselves excessive amounts for doing so and leaving society to pick up the costs. He urged business schools to mend the errors of their ways and develop more ethical business models, otherwise the corporate world would destroy itself.

*Source: Simon Caulkin, **Management Today**, Nov 2004*

Business ethics need to be defined and taught

Although there are many highly ethical people running companies, some are not ensuring that their own standards of behaviour are being applied throughout their organisations. In some cases, they are relying on business ethics to permeate the company via some form of osmosis. Unfortunately this is not enough for a variety of reasons. First, a significant proportion of school leavers are joining companies having had very limited moral education either from school or home. People are now getting into management positions with a minimal appreciation of acceptable business behaviour. Second, the personal targets given to individuals may well give rise to conflicts with good corporate behaviour. Third, it is a fact of life that little gets done in a company for its own sake. If the executive want their employees to behave in a particular way they must define that behaviour, teach it, monitor its implementation and provide rewards/sanctions for compliance/failure, just as they would with any other business requirement.

Strictly legal versus ethical best practice

When considering corporate behaviour, companies can essentially adopt one of two approaches – the Strictly Legal or Ethical Best Practice:

- ◆ The **strictly legal** approach has the advantage of relative clarity. It is compulsory and it is the standard to which most of the competition will work. Within this approach, a company may additionally have to decide whether to work to the 'letter of the law' or to the more onerous 'spirit of the law'.

- ◆ The **ethical best practice** approach is likely to require an even higher standard of behaviour than strict legal compliance. Although much of a country's legal framework is based on a view of an ethical best practice position (though perhaps of some years ago, or even of a previous generation), many laws and regulations lag behind and fall short of current ethical best practice and expectations. A company opting for the ethical best practice approach to behaviour may thus find itself at a disadvantage relative to the competition. Higher standards of behaviour usually have a higher cost, at least in the short term.

Turn up the heat

It is no mystery now why Enron collapsed. Created as an ordinary Texan company to pipe oil, it decided to trade it too. But then it decided to trade almost anything, from metals to bandwidth and even weather futures. Those businesses, set up as more than 3,000 associated partnerships, lost a fortune. The results were kept at arm's length from the main accounts; Enron used questionable accounting techniques to record 'profits' the associated businesses had made in its results, but their losses were largely invisible. When the accounts had to be revised last autumn to take account of certain losses that triggered repayment clauses on its debts the giant crashed.

On Thursday Alan Greenspan, Chairman of the US federal reserve, in testimony to Congress condemned Enron's accounting practices as 'egregious'. He called for tighter rules on 'corporate governance', arguing that an orderly market economy needs public trust in companies. In strong language he concluded, 'we are not an economy that takes erosion of reputation as a minor question'.

*Extract from editorial, **The Times**, 26 January 2002*

We're sorry, Citigroup tells staff

Citigroup, the world's biggest bank, yesterday issued a humiliating apology to its staff after a bond trading coup in August that sparked investigations by regulators across Europe. In a memo, distributed by email, head of global capital markets Tom Maheras said: 'As an industry leader, Citigroup is committed to holding itself to the highest standards in its business practices... we did not meet our standards in this instance and, as a result, we regret having executed this transaction... Unfortunately, we failed to fully consider its impact on our clients, other market participants, and our regulators... We need to be sure that in whatever we do, we fully consider the impact of our actions on our clients and the markets. We must exercise sound judgement, know our markets and our clients well and act in their best interests.'

The US bank's reputation has taken a battering as a result of a series of scandals. It paid $120m last year as punishment for aiding Enron in its plot to disguise debts a few months after contributing to a $1.4b settlement for issuing what the US watchdogs described as 'fraudulent"research.

*Extract from news article, **Daily Telegraph**, 15 September 2004*

And more...

Citigroup had to close its private banking operation in Japan in 2004 after allegedly doing business with organised crime and money launderers. When investigated by the Japanese regulator (FSA) it, 'provided responses that differed from the truth'. The group chief executive had to make this formal apology, 'I sincerely apologise to the customers and public for the company's failure to comply with legal and regulatory requirements in Japan.' He went on to say that senior staff had 'put short-term profits ahead of the bank's long-term reputation.'

*Source: **Financial Times**, 28 November 2004*

The changing attitude to ethical behaviour and legal compliance

" Over a long career in law I have observed a subtle shift in the attitude towards regulation. At one time we could rely on the majority of professional people not to behave in a certain way because it was generally considered to be unethical. Now, many seem to think that any behaviour is acceptable provided that it is not specifically proscribed by regulation – whether it is ethical or not. The rider to this is that some professionals are actively looking for loopholes in regulation to extend the limits of what they can do. As a result, regulation is having to be increased in volume and complexity to keep pace. "

Dudley Dean, Lawyer

❝❝ Again and again in America we have the problem that whether corporations obey the law or not is a matter of whether it's cost effective. If the chance of getting caught and the penalty are less than it costs to comply, our people think of it as being just a business decision. ❞❞

Robert Monk
*quoted in **The Corporation**, Joel Bakan*

❝❝ The people who run corporations have a legal duty to shareholders, and that duty is to make money. Failing this duty can leave directors and officers open to being sued by shareholders…. Corporate law thus casts ethical and social concerns as irrelevant, or as stumbling blocks to the corporation's fundamental mandate. ❞❞

Robert Hinkley
How Corporate Law Inhibits Social Responsibility
Business Ethics Jan – Feb 2002

There's a difference between legal and right

In 2002, Nestlé harmed its reputation by trying to recover $6m from the impoverished Ethiopian government. The debt was many years old, and related to a previous government regime. The stance adopted by the company was at odds with its self-promoted 'caring' image. It was compounded when Nestlé, instead of backing down gracefully, attempted to justify its action as 'a matter of principle'.

It did eventually drop the claim, but by then the damage to its reputation had been done.

*Ronald J Alsop, **The 18 Immutable Laws of Corporate Reputation***

Reasons for adopting the ethical best practice approach may vary.

1. It is the right thing to do

Despite their generally negative image, business managers come from a cross-section of society and are, on average, no less or more moral than anyone else. They generally want to 'do the right thing', although they may come under considerable pressure to do otherwise.

2. Ethical business is good business

There is a view expressed by some commentators that it is always in a company's best interest to adopt the ethical best practice approach – that ethical business is good business. This is obviously true in some areas; the Co-operative Bank's ethical investment policy has attracted many customers. However, it is likely that initiatives like this are probably only going to be niche opportunities, at least in the short term.

We believe that, in most cases, ethical best practice is indeed good business, but primarily from the long-term perspective. The ethical best practice approach would usually fail conventional cost-benefit analysis unless the full extent of reputational risk is factored into the equation. This is compromised by the fact that, in the UK and USA the normal corporate planning horizon seldom exceeds three years. If more companies took a truly long-term view and placed a proper value on their reputation (and took commensurate steps to protect it) higher standards of corporate behaviour would be likely to result.

Having a proper understanding of the value of reputation should lead to improved corporate behaviour

---

A simple ethical test for a business decision

1. **Transparency**: Do I mind others knowing what I have decided to do?
2. **Effect**: Who does my decision affect or hurt?
3. **Fairness**: Would my decision be considered fair by those affected?

Institute of Business Ethics

The reputational challenges of international business

For international companies, the adoption of ethical best practice may become a more complex exercise than that for those operating in a single country. Nevertheless, for a company wishing to protect its global reputation it is something that simply should not be ignored, The behaviour of its staff, suppliers and business partners has a significant positive of negative impact on its reputation, irrespective of where they are located.

The issues arising from operating in different cultures are not new. An old saying, 'When in Rome, do as the Romans do' suggests that some of the dilemmas involving international trade were recognised at least two millennia ago. However, the combination of the rapid increase of international economic activity, combined with better communications, has highlighted some of the difficulties that exist. More organisations are coming face to face with potentially damaging situations such as the exploitation of less developed countries (eg 'pillaging' of natural resources, low wages, child labour, poor working conditions), or benefiting from the use of different standards of behaviour in different countries (eg endemic corruption and differing legal standards). With television, the internet, investigative journalism and the activities of NGOs, any questionable business behaviour can be quickly placed before the public, with the attendant risk of reputational damage.

One issue that seems to attract more attention than most is environmental damage in the developing world. Many of the largest global companies are closely monitored by NGOs such as Green Peace and Friends of the Earth, and have to be acutely aware of the reputational consequences of their activities. Some behave well, but others have little regard for their host communities and use their substantial local influence to protect their interests. This was succinctly described by Richard Pettinger in his book, *Global Organizations*.

Environmental management

 Environmental management is a key feature of corporate citizenship and responsibility. No organization likes to be considered bad at managing this part of the business. Those that do take expedient, rather than responsible, approaches and counteract these with extensive public relations campaigns among politicians, the media, and other influential groups (in the dominant economies of the USA, the EU and Japan). Ultimately, there will only be radical changes in global organization approaches to these issues when it is made in their interests to do so, and when it runs counter to their interests not to do so. This depends on global regulation and enforcement of specific rules, together with trading penalties including restrictions on activities. Because of the extent of global organization influence, the lead for this is going to have to come from the companies themselves.

Richard Pettinger, **Global Organizations**

Determining standards of behaviour that are applicable across all parts of a global organisation is a major challenge. The best and most useful advice usually given is for the organisation 'to stick to its core values' and apply them as far as is practicable within the local context. Clearly, any organisation should comply with at least the minimum legal requirements in every country in which it operates. The limitation with this approach is that the law may differ between countries, and in some places is extremely lax or even silent in critical aspects. The question that then arises is whether or not there are commonly acceptable standards of business conduct that might be suitably implemented across most of the world?

Need to define and then stick to your core values

This was the extremely complex subject tackled in 1993 by *An Interfaith Declaration: a Code of Ethics on International Business for Christians, Muslims and Jews*. Although it addresses business ethics primarily from the standpoint of the three great monotheist religions, the underlying tenets of these religions also underpin acceptable morality in much of the world. As such it is an extremely useful starting point for any organisation wishing to safeguard its reputation through ethical behaviour in a global context, or indeed nationally, across multiple cultures.

The aim of the Declaration was to provide an ethical basis for international business, involving principles and guidelines for practice, to help business people, traders and investors identify the role they and their organisations perform in the communities in which they operate. It also gives guidance in resolving some of the dilemmas that arise in day to day business. It was compiled by a working group of eminent scholars, clerics and business people following a comprehensive review of their respective religions.

Much to everyone's surprise, the three religions found that they had far more in common than was originally believed likely, with the result that the working group was able to agree and publish the Declaration. The Declaration is based on a shared concern for the fundamental principles of:

◆ **justice**: conduct, fairness, exercise of authority in maintenance of right;
◆ **mutual respect**: consideration for others; reciprocal regard; self interest only has a place in the community in as much as it takes into account the interests of others;
◆ **stewardship**: man as a steward or trustee, with responsibility for the protection and preservation of the world around him; and
◆ **honesty**: truthfulness, reliability, integrity.

The Declaration provides Guidelines for applying the fundamental principles and establishing good practice at three separate levels through:

◆ the political and economic system within which business activity takes place;
◆ the policies and strategies of organisations which engage in business;
◆ the behaviour of individual employees in the context of their work.

The Guidelines represent a clear and well-grounded starting point for any company seeking to establish its own code of ethics.

The working group emphasised however that the application of ethical principles is a matter of personal judgement rather than rules; a code can only set standards. Moreover, in many instances in real life, there are no absolute right or wrong answers.

The Guidelines section of the Declaration is reproduced in Appendix 1. The full text is available from the Institute of Business Ethics.

There is little doubt that the Interfaith Declaration is, potentially, a very valuable piece of cultural research work for international companies. It is disappointing therefore that it was not widely discussed in business circles when it was first published. Perhaps the title, which implied a religious aim, was too off-putting for the modern market. However, anyone interested in understanding stakeholder expectations on a global scale would be well advised to adopt some of its timeless and border-less standards.

That some major companies overtly disregard such basic ideas is an indictment of the myopia of management, of how little they value their reputation, and of how 'careless' they are of the future success of the organisation over the longer term. Surely international business has moved on from the time of Cecil Rhodes?

A 'rationale' for colonialism

"" We must find new lands from which we can easily obtain raw materials and at the same time exploit the cheap slave labour that is available from the natives of the colonies. The colonies would also provide a dumping ground for the surplus goods produced in our factories. ""

Cecil Rhodes, the 19th century colonialist, quoted in
The Ecologist *22, no.4, 1992*

A Rhodes-like lack of concern for ethical standards is not limited to businesses operating in far flung, or less developed, countries. As has so clearly been demonstrated by the recent corporate scandals in the US (Enron, Worldcom, Tyco, etc), and the behaviour of participants in the investment markets, particularly during the long bull market leading to the e-bubble, but continuing well beyond the end of the bull market (eg the US mutual funds scandal), bad behaviour can just as well occur in 'home' territories and developed countries.

Ethics in the City of London

Richard Lambert, former editor of the *Financial Times*, attributes falling ethical standards in the City of London to the following.

♦ Cultural and institutional changes following the Big Bang in 1986 resulted in companies getting bigger and the disappearance of a common sense of identity. The City became more competitive and less honest.

♦ In the period of a long bull market followed by the e-bubble it became possible to cover up mistakes and still look like a genius.

♦ The penalties for unethical behaviour have been nothing like the rewards for cutting corners.

The US Mutual Funds Scandal

The mutual funds scandal in America is taking a heavy toll as investors pull their money out.

Putnam, one of the more high profile groups to be targeted, lost .... $30 billion (11% of funds under management) in three weeks.

Its funny how management that approved the trading practices that got the firms into trouble gave no thought to the risk to their reputation and the consequences of that if and when the truth emerged.

One would have thought after the collapse of Arthur Andersen in the wake of damage to its reputation over its involvement with Enron, financial firms would be more careful.

City Comment, **London Evening Standard***, 27 November 2003*

Our view on the key issues involved in developing and implementing a code of ethics is included in Appendix 2.

Conclusion

Management of reputational risk has to be addressed through the day-to-day operational and performance management processes operated by the company. Quite naturally, in response to a combination of 'those who shout loudest', and the ease with which things can be measured, in most companies the overwhelming control emphasis is on financial performance measures, addressing the interests of the shareholders, followed closely by customer metrics such as product quality and service, where customer focus is critical to success.

Conversely, measures relating to the interests and expectations of other stakeholders, such as the general public, regulators, suppliers and partners, that may be more behavioural and more difficult to measure, tend to be less frequent. However, the expectations of these stakeholders are the root cause of much reputational risk, and are likely to be increasingly important in the future – a factor recognised in the proposed revision of UK company law and reporting. When reputational risk is taken into consideration ethical best practice, the adoption of optimum standards of corporate behaviour and citizenship, begins to make far greater sense to the prudent business. The management of behaviour however needs a different skill set from that of managing numbers. Just like any other management issue, required behaviours need to be defined, codified, and taught, and operational management processes set up to manage and monitor them, which are linked to individuals' personal performance assessments.

Many companies do not currently have a full range of relevant, non-financial performance measures that they can use to demonstrate how they are meeting the full range of stakeholder expectations, neither do they manage the behaviour of all aspects of their business and employee actions in the same way that they manage the financial performance of the company.

While they may have elements of the necessary non-financial processes, measures, and codes, few have fully implemented them, monitor them effectively, or have linked them to a detailed analysis of stakeholder expectations. As a result, the reputational risk associated with the broad range of non-financial stakeholder expectations is not effectively being managed through existing operational management processes in many companies, leaving the company exposed to potential reputational damage.

Chapter 4

Risk management

On completing this chapter you will have begun to build an understanding as to why:

◆ in many companies risk management tends to concentrate on those pure or physical risks that are relatively easy to identify and understand, and are largely insurable (eg health and safety, natural, disasters, fire, liability, crime and other events that can lead to business interruption);

◆ where thought about reputational risk tends to fall into the 'too hard' box, or is assumed to be covered by addressing the pure or physical risks identified;

◆ in reality, insurance solutions are limited for the majority of causes of reputational risk;

◆ most specific reputational risk management activity focuses on post-event crisis management;

◆ leading consultants advocate a more systematic approach, with action before as well as after an event.

In previous chapters, we have explored the challenges faced in managing reputational risk in general; the issues presented by the range of differing stakeholder expectations that need to be taken into account; the difficulty of managing reputation through standard operational and performance management processes; and the increasing importance of ethical best practice activities in supporting a company's reputation.

In this, and the following chapter we will examine specific issues presented by the conventional risk management approach to reputational risk. We will then propose an approach to the systematic and holistic management of reputational risk that is practical, cost effective and meets the increasing legal and corporate governance obligations of directors to manage and report on all the major risks and issues facing the company.

Businesses thrive on risk. Without risk, there would be no new developments or discoveries and less opportunity for profit. In many instances, risk presents both an opportunity as well as a threat. Therefore an organisation's aim should be to manage those risks it faces, with a view to ensuring that its strategies are effectively executed and its business objectives achieved, rather than attempt to eliminate risk altogether.

Standard risk management approach

The basic approach to risk management in most companies, whether undertaken formally in a structured way, or informally, is as shown in the example diagram below. This has been taken from *A Risk Management Standard*, drawn up by the major risk management organisations in the UK.

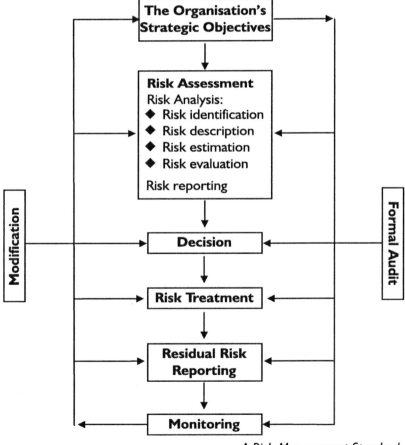

A Risk Management Standard
AIRMIC, ALARM, IRM, 2002

The basic steps consist of:

◆ identifying and assessing the significance of the risks to the achievement of the company's strategic objectives;
◆ deciding how these risks should be 'treated' (eg controlled, financed, transferred);
◆ implementing the risk treatment actions decided upon; and
◆ reviewing and monitoring the risk and risk management position over time.

It is important to note however that, with most risks, you do not try and 'manage' the risk itself, but look to manage (eg prevent or reduce the likelihood of) the incidents or events that can lead to damage, and to manage (mitigate) the impact of the damage should an event occur.

Two levels of risk management activity

Risk management will generally be utilised at two levels within a business entity.

◆ **At the Corporate level**: looking at the major strategic risks and issues that challenge the very existence or viability of the entire company, and how these are identified, assessed and managed at the corporate level (these are often not susceptible to process based controls, and are unrelated to specific physical assets).
◆ **At the Operational level**: looking at the risks in the day-to-day operations conducted by the business (directly related to the processes and assets utilised in the business) their identification, assessment and treatment.

In practice, because of the different nature of these risk types and, potentially, the different ways that they are managed, these often tend to be two separate processes – but they should be linked.

However, when it comes to formal 'risk management' structures most companies still tend to concentrate on the pure Operational risks that they face, such as:

◆ health and safety;
◆ natural disasters;
◆ fire;
◆ liability;
◆ crime; and
◆ other events that can lead to business interruption.

Companies tend to concentrate on the traditional risks

Decisions about what needs to be done about each of them are then taken individually.

Most operational risks are, as a rule, relatively easy to understand and identify, their causes are well known, and they have usually been actively managed by the company for many years. The only issue is then to assess whether management actions remain appropriate in the light of any new developments, or changes to accepted best practice. Because of the discrete nature of these risks, the management of such risks tends to be performed on a discrete basis, but within a structured 'risk management' system.

On the other hand, Corporate level risks, because of their complexity and, typically, lack of a structured process which can be managed, tend to be addressed in a variety of different ways, and often less formally than operational risks. As a result of these different approaches, in most companies the management of risk is fragmented and, in many cases, not 'joined up'.

The need for risk management to become more holistic and a more integrated part of the business process has been emphasised in the revised UK Combined Code on Corporate Governance, 2003. This makes it clear that it is the responsibility of the Board to:

◆ conduct a regular, thorough evaluation of the nature and extent of all the risks to which the company is exposed, including their frequency and impact;
◆ specify the company's risk appetite (its willingness to accept risk);
◆ agree and implement board policies on risk and control;
◆ establish prudent and effective internal controls (to enable all risks affecting the company to be assessed and managed); and
◆ at least annually, to review the effectiveness of the company's systems of internal control and risk management and formally report on them.

In addition, as mentioned in the previous chapter, proposed changes to EU company reporting regulations will require companies to produce a much more detailed description and assessment of the risks affecting the business as part of their annual reporting. It is likely that companies will be required to consider their approach to both current and future risks, whether the risks are quantifiable or not, and disclose relevant information on the company's approach to these risks to shareholders (as per the guidance produced in the UK in support of the proposed Operating and Financial Review (OFR)). This guidance made specific reference to the need to consider issues such as ethical, environmental and reputational risk in preparing such a report.

The problem with typical risk management processes and reputational risk

 Safeguarding an organisation's reputation has traditionally been overlooked largely because it has been so hard to quantify.

*John Sanders, Share the Pain, **Reinsurance** vol. 33, no 10, Apr 2003*

Like other complex risks, reputational risk is far too big a concept to try and manage as a single entity. But unlike most other risks faced by a company, it also comprises a whole range of both corporate level and operational risk elements. It therefore needs to be broken down into manageable chunks, by looking at the incidents or actions that can lead to reputational damage occurring.

Unfortunately, in any reasonably sized company, there are likely to be dozens, if not hundreds, of such potential causes of reputational damage, when you consider all the different ways in which it is possible to fail to meet the expectations of stakeholders. As a result, in a typical risk management process, reputational risk, because of its nature (extremely large and complex, largely intangible, with multiple causes across all business functions), is rarely identified as a separate risk requiring 'management' in its own right.

It is either deemed to fall into the 'too hard' box, or is assumed to be covered by addressing the other pure or physical risks identified. Some, but by no means all, of the causes of reputational risk will be addressed within the individual, pure risk assessments undertaken in a typical risk management approach, but this potentially leaves a range of causes of reputational risk, at both operational and corporate levels, that are not being addressed.

As a general rule reputational risk cannot be insured against

In the normal course of events, the financial impact of many risks can be transferred away from the company via insurance. Unfortunately, reputational loss or damage is largely uninsurable. If the original incident is an insurable peril, say an explosion in a factory, the losses from material damage and immediate, post-event business interruption may be recoverable from insurers. Nevertheless, even in these cases any damage to the company's reputation, evidenced by a fall in share value and other goodwill cannot normally be recovered.

The nearest thing to reputational risk insurance on the market is intellectual property insurance, which might include compensation for negative media reports, and crisis containment insurance, which will pay for experts to help with damage limitation. In addition, conventional Errors & Omissions insurance will pay the legal costs of defending against accusations of professional negligence by the directors. Despite the existence of these covers, in the present insurance market companies must carry the vast majority of reputational risk themselves.

As we saw in Chapter 1, at the Corporate level, reputational risk is frequently considered to be a significant issue yet, in our view, in most risk management processes there is not an appropriate structure or approach to ensure that all the causes of reputational risk have been identified, assessed and risk managed. If all the potential causes of reputational risk have not been identified, assessed,

Risk management is not joined-up for reputation

appropriately managed and linked together under the umbrella of a single risk, it is practically impossible to assess how effective the company's risk management activity is in terms of managing the overall risk to the company's reputation. Where companies have not fully joined up their risk management activity in respect of reputational risk, they are potentially in breach of the Combined Code and other corporate governance standards.

Encouragement of more active reputational risk management

A failure of companies to 'actively' manage reputational risk has been identified by an increasing number of commentators in recent years. Active Reputational Risk Management is the name of a more pro-active approach to dealing with reputational risk that has been advocated by some consultants such as the major insurance brokers Aon, Marsh and Willis and specialist reputational risk consultancies such as Brotzen Mayne.

Active reputational risk management

A conventional risk assessment framework does not always address brand and reputation risks adequately. It often produces an incomplete picture of susceptibility and escalation potential, has insufficient focus on the stakeholder considerations that drive the risks, and has insufficient system to direct and monitor risk management actions.

David Abrahams, Marsh

Senior managers cannot afford to treat one of their most valuable corporate assets in a cavalier manner. Reputation risk should be managed with the same commitment as traditional risks. Generals do not wait until the battle is looming to build their defences. In the same way, chief executives need to build their defences today. Companies should invest in reputation risk strategies and establish credit in the reputation bank before they find themselves forced to spend their way out of a crisis.

Brotzen Mayne

From their analysis, the consultants have drawn the conclusion that many companies rely too much on retrospective action, that is, post-event crisis management and damage limitation (ie PR), rather than seeking to prevent reputational damage in the first place. Their active risk management solutions involve encouraging companies to identify reputational risk issues before they occur, then to actively manage them, including both before and after the event activities.

Understanding the value of reputation too late

" Although many companies appreciate the value of reputation on a conceptual level, they tend to only think about the value of their own reputation in times of crisis. "

Ronald J Alsop, **The 18 Immutable Laws of Corporate Reputation**

Consultants can assist companies at all stages of the process. Their main added value is that they have the experience of working with similar companies, and they are able to make independent judgements on internally sensitive issues. Their methodologies and nomenclatures may differ but the following elements are usually included.

a)   Risk identification and assessment

The need to identify where and how reputational risks might occur. These could be sudden disasters, or slowly building issues that take many years to materialise. The key is to adopt what Judy Larkin called 'outside–in thinking', that is looking at the company from the perspective of each of the stakeholder groups. It requires asking the questions, 'What could go wrong?' and 'What are the stakeholders' expectations?' This may well be done as part of the wider risk assessment and management work that has to be undertaken to satisfy the broader requirements of corporate governance.

b)   Reputational risk management before the event

Acknowledging that significant reputational risk issues often arise when:
  ◆ stakeholder expectations change; or
  ◆ the company does something new.

Companies therefore need to maintain a constructive dialogue with stakeholders and, as far as possible, ensure that, what the stakeholders expect, and what companies do, and plan to do, are in alignment. It might involve modifying or abandoning certain plans, but it may equally involve educating, or otherwise seeking to influence, the stakeholders' expectations.

However, as noted earlier, reputational risk is largely uninsurable and this therefore limits the scope of insurance brokers to be able to provide insurance-based risk management solutions in this area.

c) Reputational risk management after the event (continuity and crisis management)

Acknowledging that, no matter how well a company is managed or how well its relationships are maintained, at some stage there will inevitably be an incident or the occurrence of an issue that could cause a collapse in stakeholder confidence. This is the third area where there may be significant input from consultants, usually under the title crisis or continuity management.

One longstanding corporate communications director, explained to us that, in his experience, this can be the make or break moment for a company. In a time of crisis, or close public scrutiny, the media are quick to attach labels depending on how well the company or its management conducts itself – 'accident prone', 'troubled', 'fat cats', etc. It can take years to change the label once it has stuck.

Info-tainment?

❝❝ The news media is now in the business of entertainment as well as informing the public. The journalist Kate Adie has even coined the phrase 'info-tainment' to describe the approach taken by many news editors. The implication is that every story must have a victim and a villain in order to capture the viewer's interest. And corporate reputations are often the cost. ❞❞

David Kaye, Risk Management Consultant

Companies need to acknowledge that after-the-event risk management begins much earlier than the event itself. In the time before the risk events have materialised, the company should be developing contingency plans. Obviously, such planning cannot anticipate everything that could happen, but it can get some of the logistics planned and help decide how management should react.

The characteristics of successful management of a crisis have been clearly set out below by David Brotzen.

❝❝ Successful crisis management includes:
- the demonstration of decisive remedial action;
- access to the right information;
- high speed in communications;
- a consistent corporate message;
- a full appreciation of the needs of all stakeholders;
- the ability to admit to mistakes;
- a clear recovery strategy. ❞❞

Brotzen Mayne

Reputational consultants take many forms

A number of consultants offer toolkits and support services to help companies address the risk to their reputation, and they come at the matter from a range of different angles and definitions of reputational risk. However, in our opinion, whilst they make a positive contribution in that they attempt to get reputational risk management more openly on company management's agenda, all but the very best have a tendency to fall into one of the following traps:

◆ overcomplicating matters in their detailed risk models and solutions;
◆ defining reputational risk in a way that is inconsistent with management's own view, or is incomplete in some way (eg by not addressing all aspects of reputational damage); or
◆ not going far enough in seeking to address the risk holistically and systematically.

> " Our reputational risk policy was essentially a corporate communications policy with some crisis management tagged on. It dealt with only a small proportion of causes (uncontrolled communications) and so was ineffective in either managing the risk or satisfying the regulator. "

Director, Financial Institution

At the end of the day, it is the company management themselves who need to understand and acknowledge reputational risk, and must want to manage it in a positive and effective way. Many current offerings are 'product push' based, rather than 'customer pull' based and do not do enough to encourage a deep understanding and 'ownership' of the risk by the company.

The corporate philosopher Roger Steare actually believes that something extra is needed to create that 'customer pull'.

Kick-starting more systematic reputational risk management in companies

> " Reputational risk may only be taken seriously when global accounting standards get to grip with intangibles. Until then, boards and shareholders will continue to fixate on the 20% of value they can measure. Goodwill will be left to good luck! "

Roger Steare

Conclusion

The conventional approach to risk management, with its focus mainly on the traditional physical and operational risks of a business, will almost certainly not address reputational risk in an effective or joined-up manner. Because of its complexity and mix of corporate and operational level causes, reputational risk needs to be managed from a top down perspective, in an holistic manner, across the entire business.

This approach is emphasised and confirmed by the latest developments in corporate governance and company reporting requirements, which stress the need to manage all the risks a business faces from a top down perspective, and for boards of companies to take formal ownership of, and responsibility for, the risk identification and management and internal control processes established within the company.

In the next chapter we propose a Reputational Risk Management Process, based on the standard principles of effective risk management, which addresses the concerns and inadequacies that we have highlighted so far in this book in the way that reputational risk is currently managed in most companies.

Chapter 5

A next step – A new reputational risk management process

On completing this chapter you will have begun to build an understanding as to why:

◆ responsibility for reputation should be formally owned by the CEO;

◆ responsibility for running a systematic reputational risk management process should be assigned to a senior executive with the appropriate skills and influence;

◆ the process has similarities to any other management change programme and will require a similar approach;

◆ the process will involve: understanding stakeholder expectations; determining company policy; identifying and prioritising causes of risk; identifying and implementing appropriate controls; and finally, integrating with the existing risk management framework;

◆ in order to satisfy corporate governance requirements, the risk should be reviewed and monitored as a single entity.

Having so far looked at how reputational risk is managed in a typical company, we feel that, given its significance and complexity, the typical approach of:

◆ a lack of clear ownership and accountability for reputation management;

◆ a lack of a full and clear understanding of all stakeholders' needs and expectations, and how the company intends to respond to them;

◆ a lack of a full understanding of all the potential causes of reputational damage; and

◆ fragmentary risk management activity in relation to reputational risk, together with a tendency to rely on post-event crisis management

... is not adequate. Not least, because such an approach gives no clarity that reputational risk is clearly understood, nor that it is being managed in a holistic and systematic way. As a result, we suggest that most companies are not compliant with the latest corporate governance requirements to have adequate and appropriate risk management and control systems in place.

Taking the best of the proactive approaches proposed by the consultants, and looking to address some of the problems identified previously, we propose the following process to establish 'best practice' reputational risk management:

Reputational risk management process

Reputational risk should be actively managed as a single, complex risk and have the appropriate resources allocated to its management. This will address the spirit of the UK Combined Code and proposed UK Company Law reforms.

The model (opposite) is founded on our new definition of reputational risk:

Reputational Risk =   Failure to meet stakeholders' reasonable expectations of an organisation's performance and behaviour.

1.   CEO to assume ownership of reputation

In this book, we have attempted to show that reputation is the essence of an organisation. Everyone who works there should have a vested interest in preserving the good name, but we are not advocating that they can actually 'own' the reputation. In practice, only one person should have overall accountability for it and ensure that it is appropriately managed. That person is the chief executive.

The CEO should own the corporate reputation

Many CEOs reading this book will probably be saying to themselves, 'Yes, my organisation does face significant reputational risk challenges, but what should I be doing about it?'

The options are basically to:

1. *ignore* it and hope it will go away, then *react* if and when something happens; or

2. attempt to *manage* it using some sort of systematic process.

Reputational Risk =   Failure to meet stakeholders' reasonable expectations of an organisation's performance and behaviour.

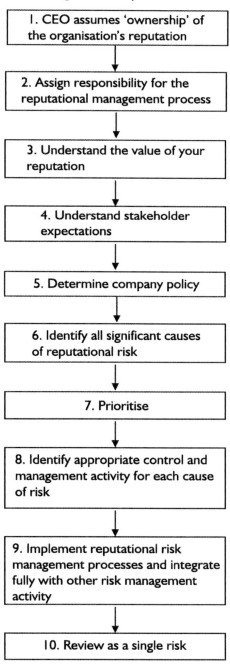

1. CEO assumes 'ownership' of the organisation's reputation

2. Assign responsibility for the reputational management process

3. Understand the value of your reputation

4. Understand stakeholder expectations

5. Determine company policy

6. Identify all significant causes of reputational risk

7. Prioritise

8. Identify appropriate control and management activity for each cause of risk

9. Implement reputational risk management processes and integrate fully with other risk management activity

10. Review as a single risk

The first option can be fatal. Reacting after the event may possibly be too late to salvage the situation. The second option, systematic management, seems to be the logical response, but is fraught with difficulties as it may require significant changes to the way that the organisation is managed and controlled.

Machiavelli may not have had much to contribute towards ethical corporate governance but he certainly knew a lot about the problems of leadership.

The challenge of change

> There is nothing more difficult to plan, more doubtful of success, nor more dangerous to manage than the creation of a new system. For the initiator has the enmity of all who would profit by the preservation of the old institutions, and merely lukewarm defenders in those who should gain by the new ones.

Niccolo Machiavelli (1469-1527)

However, if we consider the critical success factors associated with major change programmes, certain fundamentals emerge that should be common to implementing a reputational risk management process in most organisations.

2. Assign responsibility for the reputational risk management process

Responsibility for the reputational risk management process must be clearly allocated to a senior executive of the company, with the time, skills and authority to manage it effectively. As part of the allocation process, a decision will need to be made as to how performance in this role will be measured and assessed.

As we have seen in earlier chapters, reputational risk is spread across all the company's activities, functions and behaviours. As a result, the executive responsible must have the breadth of vision and the ability to influence the conduct of all aspects of the company's activities. The executive could be the existing risk manager, although in many cases today this position may lack sufficient seniority.

In some very large companies the executive assigned responsibility might wish to select a multidisciplinary team to support him, although this poses a real danger of creating a reputation 'industry'.

3.   Understand the value of your reputation

A mechanism needs to be established to assess and understand the 'value' of the company's current reputation, both in financial terms and in non-financial measures.

◆ Financial measures may include: the difference between the value of tangible assets and the company's market value or the 'value' of being able to raise capital at a different rate from other companies.

◆ Non-financial measures may or may not have clear metrics (ie some may be judgmental). One way of arriving at such measures is to assess both the direct and indirect impacts on the company if certain events occurred, eg a botched takeover, failure to deliver on plans, a messy court or industrial tribunal case.

In certain circumstances the financial measure of the value of a company's reputation may be zero or even negative, where stakeholders value the company at less than the value of its assets. This should not stop management seeking to manage reputation in a positive way. The challenge in such a case is to create a positive value for the company's reputation, then seek to protect and increase that value over time.

Only when a company has a reasonable understanding of the value of its reputation can it begin to think logically about what it might do to either enhance that value, or protect it from damage.

4.   Understand stakeholder expectations

As we have discussed in some detail in earlier chapters, companies have a range of stakeholders who may have significantly different expectations of a company's performance and behaviour. The company needs to fully understand: who all its current stakeholders are; what their specific needs and expectations of the company are; and also consider how their expectations are likely to change

Need to understand the stakeholders' expectations

and develop in the future. This analysis should specifically include consideration of any special interest groups, NGOs, etc who could target the company in the future.

A structured process should be established to research and analyse all the company's stakeholder expectations, and their potential to change over time. Only when a company fully understands all its stakeholders' expectations can it begin to consider what it should do in response.

5. Make a formal decision on company policy

Once the value of its reputation has been defined and the expectations of stakeholders clearly established, the company is then in a position to **make explicit decisions on how it wishes to manage its reputation**, both generally and in specific areas, and how the company should address specific stakeholder expectations, to protect or grow that reputational value. This may be:

◆ do everything possible to meet fully, or exceed, specific expectations;
◆ do the minimum necessary to avoid serious problems with specific expectations of stakeholders;
◆ do not take any particular action to try and meet specific expectations, but watch out for problems arising from those stakeholders should expectations not be met in some way; or
◆ some other choice of action.

The key issue is that it should be **a positive decision** on how the company will seek to address each set of stakeholder expectations, **clearly linked to the protection or enhancement of the company's reputational value**.

A thorough understanding of stakeholder expectations, combined with an understanding of the actual or desired value of a company's reputation, is likely to:

◆ demonstrate the need for many companies to operate in a socially more responsible way than they do at present; and
◆ confirm the benefits of adopting an ethical best practice approach.

---

6. Assess the causes of reputational risk

As previously stated, reputational risk is far too big and complex a concept to try and manage on a day-to-day basis as a single entity, despite the fact that it needs to be managed as a single entity at the corporate level. It therefore needs to be broken down into manageable chunks. As with any risk, you do not try and manage the risk itself, but look to manage (eg prevent) the incidents or events that can lead to damage, and to manage (mitigate) the impact of the damage should an event occur.

Using the decisions made in Stage 5 above to focus the work, a detailed assessment of the potential causes of reputational damage needs to be made. The key is to identify events, actions, or failures to act that would adversely impact the company's reputation, bearing in mind the company's decision on how it intends to address specific stakeholder expectations.

There are likely to be dozens, if not hundreds, of such potential causes of reputational damage, and some form of reasonableness or materiality test will need to be built into the process to avoid unnecessary work.

7. Assess the relative importance of the various causes of risk

Having identified the potential causes of risk, each cause then needs to be assessed in terms of:

◆ **probability** – how likely is this event?; how often might it occur?, and
◆ **impact** – should it occur, how much damage (whether financial or non-financial) will it do to the company's reputation?

This will allow decisions to be made in terms of relative importance of different causes of risk, and therefore how much effort or money it is worth allocating to managing each cause.

8. Identify the 'management' action required for each cause of risk

For each cause of risk a decision on what are the required management actions must be taken. This can include a decision to take no specific management action, if the cause of risk is deemed insignificant, but this must be clearly flagged, and be subject to review and challenge on a regular basis.

Actions required may include the need to manage or control a range of 'soft' issues such as ethics, trust, corporate and individual behaviours, social responsibility and the creation of 'advance warning' processes to identify issues at an early stage.

9. Integrate with existing risk management processes and management controls

Having identified the causes of risk and required actions to specifically manage reputational risk, these then need to be implemented and integrated with existing risk management and operational control processes. Some of the causes of reputational risk will already be identified and incorporated into the company's existing risk management structures. Similarly, some of the required reputational risk management actions will already be in place within the different business functions. Any causes of risk or management actions not already incorporated within existing processes must then be implemented. This is where the ability to influence across the entire business is critical, as this may involve implementing new management or control processes in parts of the business not directly controlled by the overall 'owner' of reputational risk. Once implemented and integrated, the day-to-day monitoring can be delegated to the existing risk management function.

Cross-business influence is critical

10. Review as a single risk

All causes of risk associated with reputational risk should be coded within the risk management reporting process so that all the causes of reputational risk, and their associated controls, can be extracted and reported as a separate group to the reputational risk owner.

Such a process may take a fair amount of time and effort to set up if there is not much there to start from. In particular, understanding: the value of the organisation's reputation, the true expectations of each stakeholder group, the causes of reputational risk; and, establishing appropriate and effective measures of non-financial performance and behaviour may be particularly complex, and may require external consultancy support. But once set up and operating as an integrated part of the organisation's normal activity, the process should be relatively straightforward to operate thereafter. The main ongoing challenges will involve the creation of radar/early warning systems, to monitor changes to stakeholder expectations for all stakeholder groups and identify new or changing potential causes of reputational risk, and the regular review of the effectiveness of risk management processes in place to manage the risk. With current and proposed changes to corporate governance, company law and company reporting, most organisations will be required to perform such activity (at least to some extent) in the near future to satisfy their compliance obligations.

Alignment of reputational risk management with strategic objectives

If it is to work, the approach to managing reputational risk must be seen to be completely aligned and consistent with the achievement of the organisation's strategic objectives. Any apparent conflicts will need to be identified and rectified before an effective system of risk management can be put in place. This may mean a reappraisal of some of the organisation's existing strategic objectives, once a full understanding and assessment of reputational risk has been achieved (eg focus on short-term or long-term performance). And, as noted previously, existing performance measures and incentive schemes may need to be amended to ensure that they encourage the performance and behaviours required to effectively manage reputational risk.

But surely this is just standard risk management?

It is, but reputational risk, as we have explained previously, is significantly more complex and far-reaching than most other threats managed by a typical risk management function.

Compared with 'standard' risks, for reputational risk:

◆ The causes of risk are generally:
- far more numerous;
- far more complex;
- driven by more judgmental, intangible factors (eg stakeholder expectations, behaviour), that can and will change over time;
- relate to many different elements of the company's activities at the same time; and
- bring in new 'soft' concepts that may not be part of the existing risk management structures (eg behaviour, trust).

◆ The risk management actions can:
- involve company-wide initiatives (codes of practice, ethics);
- relate to relatively intangible, difficult to measure concepts (behaviour, trust, integrity);
- require different skills and mind-sets to conventional control activity; and
- include long-term actions, which need to be managed over many years (building trust, developing environmentally friendly processes, etc), rather than being all essentially short-term.

◆ The function of pulling together the overall, residual risk position (after action has been taken to treat the risk) is considerably more complex, given the different stakeholder expectations, and how various stakeholders may react should their expectations not be met.

A typical multi-divisional organisation

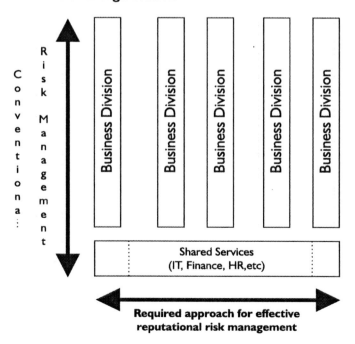

91

◆ Because of the significance of the risk and its widespread nature, there is a constant need to monitor for changes in stakeholder expectations and to re-assess the adequacy and appropriateness of management actions to meet those expectations.

◆ Reputation needs to be managed 'across' the company, not vertically down through the company's various silos, in the way that most other risks are managed.

Proactive, systematic reputational risk management is likely to be critical to the long-term success of most organisations, and this is increasingly being recognised through revisions to corporate governance, company law and reporting requirements. It can be done with sufficient understanding, communication and management drive, and ought to be at, or near the top of, every board's agenda (in the same way that it is at, or near the top of, executive concerns surveys).

A few leading companies are already well advanced in actively managing their reputations, in order to create long-term benefit.

The question is, can your organisation afford to do otherwise?

The two small surveys that end this chapter suggest that even the largest, most respected companies in the UK still have some way to go in effectively managing reputational risk, with particular regard to:

◆ fully assessing and understanding all aspects of reputational risk;

◆ establishing effective control and management processes for dealing with reputational risk;

◆ clearly defining and allocating responsibility for managing and protecting the organisation's reputation; and

◆ monitoring the organisation's performance in meeting stakeholders' expectations in respect of the employees, suppliers/business partners, and society at large/NGOs stakeholder groups.

If, as suggested by these surveys, the best have still some way to go to effectively manage reputational risk, there must be a reasonable expectation that the rest have even further to go.

A view from the best risk managed companies

In the spring of 2004, The Cullen Centre for Risk and Governance at Glasgow Caledonian University, with the support of AIRMIC, undertook a small on-line survey of risk managers from major UK corporations.

The aim was to see how some of the best risk managed companies were dealing with reputational risk.

Key points from the survey included the following.

All respondents considered reputational risk to be one of the most important risks faced by their organisation, but at the same time:

◆ 53% believed that their organisation had not fully assessed all aspects of reputational risk;

◆ 41% did not have control and management processes fully in place for dealing with reputational risk;

◆ 53% had not clearly defined and allocated responsibility for managing and protecting the organisation's reputation.

The position regarding monitoring reputational risk through the use of metrics to measure the organisation's performance in meeting stakeholders' expectations were somewhat patchy:

◆ with 81% having metrics for shareholders and 75% for customers and government/regulators;

◆ but only 56% for employees and suppliers/business partners, and 44% for society at large and NGOs.

On a stronger note, it seems that formal written policies and charters are now common in large corporates, such as those surveyed:

Compliance with law and regulation	100%
Ethics/conduct	94%
Risk management	87%
Environment	82%
Corporate social responsibility	77%
Customer charters	71%

Audience voting on reputational risk
UK Institute of Risk Management (IRM) Forum, 2004

The authors presented some thoughts based on the content of this book at the 2004 IRM Forum, and then asked the audience to vote using electronic keypads on a range of questions concerning reputational risk. The audience consisted primarily of professional risk managers working within large organisations and consultants/ advisors on risk management.

The results show a similar position to the AIRMIC survey.

73% were not aware that their organisation had ever attempted to formally assess or measure the value of its reputation.

53% did not know who, if anyone, formally owns their organisation's reputation.

59% did not believe that their organisation had formally assessed the expectations of all its principal stakeholders.

72% did not believe that their organisation had a systematic process for managing its reputation.

Yet, as with the AIRMIC survey, most (between 64% and 82%) of the organisations represented had formal written charters/codes of conduct for each of: regulatory compliance, ethics/conduct, risk management, environment, and customers.

Chapter 6

Lessons from real life

On completing this chapter you will have:

◆ gained additional insight into some of the causes of reputational damage experienced by real companies in recent times; and
◆ begun to understand some of the lessons learned from such examples.

Throughout this book, a number of real-life examples of companies, which have failed to live up to their stakeholders' expectations, have been highlighted. Deeper analysis of such cases allows us to suggest lessons that might be learned from such events, and to make recommendations for good practice that may be taken on board by others, in order to prevent reputational damage in future.

Many of these lessons are generic, and not limited to the industry sector in which they originally occurred.

The Case of Shell

The damage done to oil giant Shell by overstating its proven oil and gas reserves underlines a number of important lessons for those wishing to manage reputational risk. In particular, it demonstrates how a complacent, possibly naïve, corporate culture allowed a technical debate to escalate into a crisis of confidence in the management. Unfortunately, Shell clearly had not learned from the hostile media reaction to its decision to sink the Brent Spar oil rig a few years before.

A major part of the value creation ability of any oil company is the location of new oil and gas reserves to replace the oil and gas that it extracts. These reserves of oil and gas still in the ground form a key part

---

in ascertaining the value of the company overall. In large companies, such as Shell, these reserves can represent many billions of dollars but, because of their nature, the amounts of unextracted oil and gas in such reserves cannot be easily verified by investors.

Because of this uncertainty, the US Securities and Exchange Commission (SEC) established a set of rules and guidelines for the calculation and reporting of 'proven' and 'unproven' oil and gas reserves for oil companies listed in the US. Proven reserves represent reserves where there is a high certainty as to the quantity of oil and gas in the ground and the proportion that can be extracted within a reasonable timeframe. Unproven reserves represent oil and gas finds where there is less certainty over the volume in the ground and/or how much could be commercially extracted. Clearly, unproven reserves have a significantly lesser 'value' as far as investors are concerned, than proven reserves.

Shell had Stock Exchange listings in New York, London and Amsterdam. Yet for a number of years prior to 2004, the company would appear to have used a different approach to that specified by the SEC rules for calculating and publicly reporting proven oil and gas reserves.

The problem was that Shell's own interpretation of proven reserves differed significantly from that of the regulators and over time the gap had widened. The company then made an announcement that it would initiate a review, so triggering concern among the shareholders about the value of their investment. The SEC and the FSA (the equivalent UK regulator) responding to the shareholders began to look at the stated reserves in more detail. Both regulators became uneasy and gave the company indications that they felt the figures were incorrect in both 2000 and 2001, followed up by stronger warnings that its proven reserve figures appeared false or misleading in 2002 and 2003. These concerns appear to have initially been rejected by Shell management.

In January 2004 Shell shocked the investment markets by announcing that its proven oil and gas reserves were 20% less than it had previously reported. It then made matters worse by revising the figure a further three times, before finally admitting that it had overstated its reserves by 23% - almost 4.5 billion barrels - valued at something in the order of $50-100 billion at market prices.

Shell commissioned an independent review to identify how the problem had arisen. This review was critical of the Chairman of the Committee of Managing Directors (who had previously been Shell's Head of Exploration) and his successor as Head of Exploration. They were both obliged to step down, to be followed shortly afterwards by the Finance Director. Particularly damaging was the disclosure of a series of internal emails including one in which the Head of Exploration told the Chairman that he was 'sick and tired of lying' about the oil reserves.

Shell honoured the employment contracts of the dismissed directors and so the Chairman received £1m and the Head of Exploration 3.8m euro in termination payments. The Chairman also became immediately entitled to his pension of £564,070 a year, though the Head of Exploration must wait until 2015 to collect his annual pension of 385,000 euro.

In July 2004 Shell was fined $120 million by the SEC after an inquiry found that the company had violated record-keeping and anti-trust rules in relation to the reporting of proven reserves. The company also had to pay a fine of £17 million imposed by the FSA in relation to the same matter. When describing these fines, the *Daily Telegraph* said, 'on top of all this comes the loss of Shell's reputation – its ultimate hidden reserve'.

The reputational damage may have had limited impact at the petrol pump but it has had immense repercussions within the company and throughout the investment community. One indicator is that the company fell from being ranked 5th to 64th in the annual list of *UK's Most Admired Companies*.

Jeroen van der Veer, the new Chairman of the Committee Managing Directors given the task of trying to restore the company's credibility has said, 'Shell people understand we have a reputation problem, even though the issues have happened in (only) one part of the organisation'. He has taken firm action including:

◆ sweeping away the complex ownership and management structures in favour of a unified £100 bn company listed in London but with its headquarters in The Hague;
◆ providing new focus and corporate objectives;
◆ changing the management culture to increase transparency and accountability,
◆ scrapping staff bonus schemes linked to oil reserves, as he believed that they provided an inappropriate incentive, which could lead to the exaggeration of such reserves.

Lessons learned from the Shell scenario include the following:

1.   'See ourselves as others see us'

A former senior manager of Shell gave us a fascinating description of the corporate culture that existed at the time of the crisis. He felt the management to be fundamentally honest. However, on the debit side, it was extremely inward looking and self-confident to the point of arrogance. (Some observers likened it to the Kremlin.) With its hundred years of experience, there was little the company didn't know about the oil business. The old slogan, 'You can be sure of Shell' went right through the corporate DNA. The problem with such an attitude is that it can cause a company to lose touch with external perceptions. Shell completely overlooked the fact that society had moved on and was no longer prepared to take on trust what large corporations told them.

When the reserving issue arose, he believed that a fierce internal technical argument flared up and continued for many months on what was the best way of closing the gap that had arisen. Unfortunately it became highly personalised and acrimonious as demonstrated by the infamous email which was an exasperated plea to stop arguing and get the matter resolved. The company became even more introspective and lost sight of the need to consider how the rest of the world viewed it. Shell totally failed to manage the issue as a potential crisis of confidence.

2.   Admit mistakes quickly and gracefully

Shell's overstatement of its reserves appears to have occurred over an extended period. It should not have allowed the situation to develop. As soon as a company discovers that it has a serious problem it should come clean at the earliest possible moment, and then actively manage the communication process to minimise damage. Procrastination, denial, or even worse, appearing to have an admission forced out into the open, is futile in the long run. The inevitable loss of stakeholder trust will far outweigh any short-term gains. Unless they have been kept informed, the media will usually conclude that there has been a cover up, irrespective of what has really happened.

Perhaps the one positive thing about Shell's conduct over this period was its willingness to open its books to the regulators. This cooperation ultimately proved to be an important factor in limiting the size of the fines.

3.   Don't be seen to reward failure

The reputational damage associated with the failure of senior management was undoubtedly compounded by the size of the exit packages given to the Chairman and Head of Exploration. One City editor summed up shareholders' anger by saying 'These two did screw up. They had to go, but a seven figure award for doing so is pretty eye-watering'. Of course, leading companies like Shell must provide competitive contracts of employment in order to attract the best talent but this does have a severe downside when things go wrong. The giving of huge payoffs to executives, who have clearly failed to perform their duties effectively, does nothing to help restore a company's reputation. It merely reinforces an impression that management places their own interests before those of other stakeholders – it rubs salt into the wound.

4. Incentivisation must encourage the desired corporate behaviour

We may never know what actually drove the directors to ignore the SEC rules for so long – it is quite possible that some directors hoped the problem would simply go away when new reserves were discovered. Nevertheless, the very existence of bonus schemes that were linked to reserves did not inspire stakeholder confidence. The need to align incentives unambiguously with desired behaviour was obviously understood by Mr van der Veer when he introduced new company-wide bonus schemes 'to encourage staff to think enterprise-first rather than self-first'. At the same time he announced, 'Multiple scorecards will be replaced by single group scorecards, focusing on execution of strategy, delivery of operational objectives and enterprise first. Enterprise first addresses the importance of group needs over the needs of individual operating units.'

5. Ethical best practice cannot be adopted selectively – if you are going to promote such a corporate stance everyone, from the bottom to the very top, must comply

Shell was perceived as a world leader in its CSR approach, and it particularly emphasised its environmental work. It is keen to be viewed as a good neighbour. Shell's Chairman of the Committee of Managing Directors had even published a book entitled *Walking the Talk* – emphasizing the need for senior management to be totally committed to living the company's commitments to CSR, good corporate behaviour and other corporate cultural objectives, and not just pay lip service to the concepts. However, all the reputational capital built up by such positive activity is destroyed if it appears that the company tolerates contrary behaviour internally.

6. Organisations need a fully effective and functioning 'conscience'

Large, complex organisations need robust internal structures that effectively identify and manage risk, constantly monitor for deviations from approved standards, identify developing issues and problems and constructively challenge management. As part of its settlement with the SEC, Shell agreed to develop a 'comprehensive internal compliance programme'.

All companies need to take compliance with all relevant rules, regulations and standards (whether internally or externally set) seriously to protect their reputations. The larger, more complex the organisation, the stronger and more complex the compliance function needs to be. It must also have the power to assess every level of the company, up to the very top.

However, it is not enough just to have a compliance function, to work effectively this needs to be partnered with effective and enterprise-wide:

◆ corporate governance procedures; and

◆ risk identification and management procedures; and

◆ robust internal control procedures; and

◆ internal audit/checking procedures.

What would happen in your company if someone at senior level contravened some important regulation? Would you know? Would anyone have the power to challenge them? Would the whistleblower receive support and protection?

7. Directors must be vigilant at all times

Clearly not all the directors of Shell understood the technicalities of the reserve situation. However, what this case demonstrates is that, as guardians of the company's reputation, a board should take nothing for granted.

Reports should be questioned and challenged, independent views sought, and an active interest taken in every part of the organisation's activities. This is particularly an issue where matters involving significant levels of judgment, opinion or technical expertise, on behalf of the presenter of the information, are put in front of them for consideration. In other words, they should perform their duties with the same rigour that the owner/manager of a small business would with his own organisation. A small businessman has the incentive that he or she is dealing with their own money and their personal reputations are at stake. Somehow, this direct connection with the business seems to get lost as organisations grow.

One respected financial commentator writing about the Shell case, summarised it thus:

> 'The price of reputation is eternal vigilance. Eternal compliance is not the same thing. Directors must sometimes feel that they have been sentenced to it. The moral is that chairmen and directors need to mind their own businesses, if they fail in that, no reviews or reports can salvage a reputation. It cannot be replenished, like a supply of oil, or ordered and bought in from some supplier of images. It will have to be rebuilt and earned, and that takes time, if it can be done at all.'
>
> *Christopher Fildes*

The case of ValuJet

On 11 May 1996, ValuJet Flight 592 left Miami International Airport bound for Atlanta, Georgia. Approximately six minutes after take-off, the crew reported smoke in the cabin and a loss of control over the aircraft systems. The plane, a DC-9, then plunged nose first into the Florida Everglades, killing all 110 passengers and crew.

The immediate cause of the accident appeared to be a fire, initiated by one or more of the oxygen generators that had been loaded into the plane's cargo hold.

The accident immediately called into question the safety record and safety practices of ValuJet, and of other low-cost, 'no frills' airlines. The public and the media questioned whether attempts by such airlines to keep costs as low as possible had ultimately compromised passenger safety.

ValuJet's fleet of aircraft averaged 26 years of age, compared to an industry standard of 15 years. Their accident record was 14 times higher than that of American or United Airlines. Moreover, their corporate culture was likened to that of NASA, prior to the launch of the space shuttle, Challenger. Employees reported pressure to 'tow the company line' and to keep bad news to themselves, for fear that it might have an adverse effect on the financial markets.

On 18 May 1996, ValuJet was the most actively traded share on the Nasdaq, with more than 23 million traded – 10 times the normal volume. By 21 May, ValuJet stock had lost 39% of its value from the day prior to the crash and this economic decline was set to get worse.

On 17 June, ValuJet was ordered to suspend its services. Although the FAA approved the resumption of services on 30 September, passenger numbers stayed low, no matter what discounts were offered. In July 1997, just over a year after the crash, ValuJet merged with a small, Florida-based carrier called AirTran and adopted its name. For all intents and purposes, ValuJet ceased to exist.

With a change of image, a new President and CEO, the purchase of more fuel-efficient aircraft, the opening of new markets and targeting of both leisure and business customers, AirTran has proved to be a success in the competitive low-cost airline market. One of the first things the new CEO implemented was the retrofitting of smoke detection systems in every aircraft. This task was completed in 1998, two years ahead of federal requirements.

While initial media attention focused on ValuJet, and its perceived failings, it soon became apparent that other companies and agencies had contributed to the circumstances leading to the fatal crash. The official inquiry of the National Transportation Safety Board (NTSB), published in 1997, found that the fire on board flight 592 was indeed caused by one or more of the oxygen generators being activated at some point after the loading process began, but possibly as late as during the plane's take-off roll. Had a smoke/fire warning device been fitted, and activated, this would have alerted the pilots to the fire more quickly, and would have allowed them more time to land the plane. Additionally, had the plane been fitted with a fire suppression system it might have delayed the spread of the fire and, again, given the pilots time to land.

It was on this point that the first criticisms were levelled at the US Federal Aviation Administration (FAA). Following a similar incident in 1988 where, fortunately, the aircraft had been able to land safely with no loss of life, the NTSB recommended that the FAA require fire detection systems, fire extinguishing systems and better fire blocking materials be fitted in cargo compartments. At that time, the FAA said that the $300m cost was too much for the airline industry to bear, and no action was taken. In its report into the crash of flight 592, the NTSB stated that 'had the FAA required fire/smoke detection and fire extinguishment systems in class D cargo compartments, as the Safety Board recommended in 1988, ValuJet flight 592 would likely not have crashed'.

The NTSB was also critical of the FAA's system of safety inspection, particularly its failure to adequately monitor ValuJet's heavy maintenance programs and responsibilities, including ValuJet's oversight of its contractors. As a result of the investigation, the NTSB made a total of twenty-two recommendations relating to FAA practices.

While it was obvious that the crew of ValuJet flight 592 were not aware that they were transporting hazardous materials, the NTSB believed that this might not have been the first time that ValuJet had acted contrary to the authority given to it, which did not include the right to transport such materials.

What was clear was the failure of the maintenance sub-contractors, SabreTech, to properly prepare, package and identify the unexpended oxygen generators, before presenting them to ValuJet for carriage onboard flight 592. Not only were some of the canisters not completely empty, they were not fitted with safety caps, not labelled as being hazardous, and packed improperly using bubble wrap and paper towel boxes.

In early 1997, SabreTech folded. However, the company later faced criminal charges, with 110 counts of murder and 110 counts of manslaughter. The charges claimed that the deaths of the passengers and crew on flight 592 resulted from reckless indifference or gross careless disregard for human health. It was the first time in US history that criminal charges had been brought, following a civil air accident. Under the terms of a plea bargain with the Florida attorney general's office, SabreTech's parent company – Sabreliner – agreed to donate $500,000 to aviation safety programs, and the charges were dropped.

In a separate action, the company was fined $1.75m, the highest settlement the FAA had ever achieved with respect to the transportation of hazardous materials, reflecting the extreme seriousness of the case. It is estimated that SabreTech's insurers paid around $300m to settle lawsuits from the families of the victims.

Lessons learned from the ValuJet crash include:

1. Never compromise where safety is concerned

When airlines in both the US and the UK were deregulated, it paved the way for a large number of new players to enter the market. These 'no frills' operators offered reduced fares by cutting out what were seen as unnecessary extras, such as paper tickets, and by charging for food and drink services onboard aircraft. At no time did the public consider that safety might be one of the areas where corners were being cut. Companies need to ensure that they are sending out the right message to their employees.

While it is essential for an airline to be efficient if it is to compete in what is a highly aggressive marketplace, pressure on staff to ensure rapid turnaround on the ground (some low-cost carriers aim to spend only 25 minutes at the gate, between landing and take-off) must not take precedence over adequate safety. More generally, all products that human beings consume, wear or utilise, are expected to be 'safe'. The public expects 'zero risk' and the greater the potential for harm to be caused, the greater the expectation that every measure possible will be taken to protect them. When a failure relating to health and safety results in serious injury or death, damage to corporate reputation can far outweigh the cost of compensation for the individual(s) concerned.

2. Outsourcing does not get rid of risk

Although blame for the crash of ValuJet flight 592 rested with not one, but three parties – the FAA, ValuJet and SabreTech – it was the latter that generated most of the criticism for its poor staff training and unsafe practices, and ultimately faced criminal and civil charges for the deaths of the 110 people involved. Unlike ValuJet, which merged with AirTran and went on to achieve commercial success, and the FAA, which despite coming under severe criticism and losing some of its top administrators, still plays a significant role today, SabreTech suffered a complete collapse. Nonetheless, ValuJet were criticised for having failed to adequately oversee SabreTech and, according to the NTSB, this failure was a cause of the accident. ValuJet was a known brand. SabreTech was relatively unknown outside the industry in which it operated.

Although outsourcing may transfer aspects of risk, by contract, it will not transfer public perception of risk and responsibility. When a major transport accident occurs, it is the principal provider – be that an airline, rail operator or ferry company – that will attract the first wave of blame. The fact that the maintenance, or other functions that contributed to the cause of the accident, were outsourced is of little interest to the public. Full risk assessments should be conducted when decisions are taken to outsource a key corporate function, and a system of monitoring put in place to ensure that the organisation's reputation is not put at risk.

3. Manage the media

The tragedy that befell ValuJet flight 592, its passengers and crew, had an impact that went far beyond the companies and organisations that were directly involved in this event. Failures arising in one company can often lead to greater scrutiny of the wider industry in which it operates. This was the case for the airline industry as a whole, but particularly for low-cost operators, where the accusation that the offering of low fares had led to cut-backs in safety, was widely discussed. For a time this actually created an advantage for the more established airlines, whose stock values rose as those of ValuJet and other carriers fell. However, even the established airlines found that they had to increase their marketing spend in order to assure the public that no aspect of their safety was being compromised, and to distinguish themselves, in that respect, from the low-cost carriers that were under scrutiny.

Experience shows that one of the best tactics for an organisation that has suffered an incident, resulting in death and injury, is to firstly to ensure that it is looking after the victims and their families, and to make this the primary message for the media. Investigation of actions leading up to the incident and allocation of responsibility can only be done after careful inquiry. Companies that have already built up a good reputation bank, ie that have a previously clean record and are perceived to care about their employees and customers or clients, are more likely to receive favourable press when something goes wrong.

4. Role of the regulator

Regulators can come in for criticism when they are viewed as being too protective of their industry, and not sufficiently protective of their customers. The FAA came in for severe criticism for their role in the ValuJet crash and for their inadequate inspection regime, particularly with regard to maintenance of aircraft. When an industry is allowed by government to largely 'police' itself, it must ensure that it maintains the greatest level of integrity, sets high standards for all its members, and acts swiftly when one of them fails to meet expectations. If the regulatory body cannot maintain a reputation for setting and achieving exceptional standards, it may find that government takes some of the responsibility out of its hands, and legislates to ensure that adequate controls are put in place.

5. Create the right kind of corporate culture

In striving to make profits, many organisations offer staff bonuses and other financial incentives, which can result in excessive risk-taking. In the case of ValuJet, bad news was suppressed, whistle-blowing discouraged, 'blind eyes' turned to unauthorised practices. ValuJet employees were, in turn, rewarded with bonuses and incentives based on profits and company performance.

Governments in both the United States and the UK have sought to encourage, and to protect, whistle-blowers, particularly where the issues involve matters of public interest or public safety. If corporations wish to avoid incidents that will result in damaging publicity and cause detriment to their reputations, their boards must ensure that they put systems in place that will make it easy for employees to highlight any concerns that they might have, and then take any necessary action.

When it comes to responsibility for failure, the buck stops at the top. It is not acceptable for a CEO or board to claim – as was the case in the collapse of Barings Bank – that they did not know that illegitimate or unauthorised activities were being carried out by an employee. Similarly, the award of bonus payments, based on certain aspects of corporate performance, could lead to risk-taking that creates an Enron-like situation, where the achievement of personal bonuses outweighs any regard for the impact on the business as a whole.

6. Need to balance stakeholder demands

Listed companies need to provide good returns for their shareholders, if investor confidence is to be maintained. However, the demands of all the organisation's stakeholders must be considered, and met, as far as possible. In particular, the desire for profits must not conflict with the demands of safety. Although no company has unlimited resources to throw at this problem, boards must ensure that effective risk assessment and risk management procedures are put in place. If, following an incident, the company can show that they did everything that could reasonably be expected of them, under the circumstances, they will be in a better position to protect their corporate reputation than if they are shown to be lacking in some respect.

The case of Parmalat

When Calisto Tanzi formed Parmalat in 1961, the twenty-two year old Italian could scarcely have imagined the heights of success that the company would achieve. From a small, family-run food business based in the region around Parma, the Parmalat enterprise expanded to become one of the world's biggest and best-known producers of milk and dairy products, diversifying into other products such as biscuits, fruit juices and pasta sauces.

Although listed on the Milan stock exchange, Parmalat was 51% owned, and effectively controlled, by the founding Tanzi family, with Calisto Tanzi as Chairman and CEO. The company was one of the early pioneers of brand advertising, sponsoring Nikki Lauda, the racing driver, Lucciano Pavarotti, the opera singer, and Parma football club, which Tanzi purchased in 1991.

At its peak, Parmalat employed more than 35,000 people in 30 countries, with a turnover of €7.6bn ($7.2bn) in 2002. In December 2003 share trading was suspended, Calisto Tanzi resigned and was arrested, and an administrator – Enrico Bondi – was brought in to try and sort out what the US Securities and Exchange Commission subsequently described as 'one of the largest and most brazen corporate financial frauds in history'. Parmalat's debt was subsequently estimated at €14bn, eight times the €1.8bn posted in the 3rd quarter results for 2003.

Bondi's task was, firstly, to find out what went wrong. Secondly, to stave off the threat of Parmalat's short-term liquidity crisis, and thirdly, to restore the longer-term reputation of the company. At the heart of the crisis was a range of complicated financial structures, reminiscent of some of Enron's activities, that had been put in place with the complicity of a number of major Italian and international banks. Citigroup, for example, had registered an entity for Parmalat in Delaware in 1999 and called it 'Buconero' – Italian for 'black hole' – which was used to conceal borrowings and commit fraud. Citigroup has said that it regrets the choice of name, but denies any wrongdoing.

Auditors too had their part to play, with the Italian arm of Grant Thornton International verifying audited statements from a Parmalat subsidiary, Bonlat, which purported to show billions of dollars of cash balances, (that were then offset against the high levels of debt on the parent company's balance sheet), which do not appear to have existed. Parmalat's main auditors, Deloitte & Touche appear to have accepted this information, without question. In contrast, Bondi's report to the Italian industry minister in June 2004 suggests that even a back-of-the-envelope analysis using centrally available risk data published by the Bank of Italy, and Bloomberg, should have been enough to alert people that Parmalat was in trouble, as early as 1997. While the company may still have collapsed, it would have cost less money than it ultimately lost in 2003.

As far as reputational damage is concerned, the collapse of Parmalat has had a wide-reaching impact. First, has been the damage to the personal reputations of Calisto Tanzi, other members of his family, former Chief Finance Officers, internal accountants and legal counsel of Parmalat, who have variously been questioned, arrested and had their personal assets impounded by the Italian courts. By September 2004, twenty-seven people were under investigation by prosecutors for bankruptcy fraud, accounting fraud, money laundering and embezzlement. Tanzi himself has admitted siphoning as much as €800m to fund his family's travel and holiday company.

Such a massive fraud could only come about if the systems, checks and balances, in place to try and prevent such failures, had themselves failed to come up to the mark. Next in the firing line, therefore, came the reputation of the Italian authorities. Blame was put on Italy's inadequate corporate governance systems, weak regulations and tolerance of corruption. Despite a 1999 reform that imposed independent directors on the boards of Italian listed companies, large enterprises like Parmalat were allowed to opt out. Italy had also introduced laws to make false accounting a civil rather than a criminal offence, thereby downplaying the seriousness of such behaviour. Also highlighted was an alleged culture of cronyism resulting in companies with strong patriarchal leaders having boards consisting mainly of family members and friends. Italy's finance minister stated that the Parmalat affair could cost the state €11bn, with fears that damage to Italy's image and some of its most respected institutions might deter foreign investment.

Parmalat's auditors, Italaudit, the Italian arm of Grant Thornton International, had been Parmalat's long-time auditors until 1999, when Deloitte & Touche were appointed. Nonetheless, Grant Thornton continued as auditors of Bonlat, the Parmalat subsidiary at the heart of this financial scandal, and have been accused of falsely reporting Bonlat's financial position. Deloitte's unquestioning acceptance of the information provided to them has also raised questions about their honesty, professionalism and business practices. In the case of Enron their accountants – Arthur Andersen – lost clients long before the case came to court. It remains to be seen whether the reputational damage to Grant Thornton and to Deloitte & Touche has a similar effect.

Enrico Bondi estimated that Parmalat had, directly or indirectly, obtained €13.2bn from banks between December 31 1998 and December 31 2003. 80% of this was obtained from international banks, with the other 20% from Italian lenders. In contrast, Parmalat had a gross cashflow of only €1bn over the same period. Furthermore, banks had made use of the particular laws of 'tax havens' to place bonds and structure financial products that contributed to the false picture of the financial health of the group. These transactions generated huge fees for the banks. In return, they appear to have been reluctant to ask too many questions.

Respectable banks such as Bank of America, Citigroup, JP Morgan and Deutsche Bank constructed deals which allowed Parmalat to transfer funds offshore and speculate with them. While answerable to their own shareholders, they are not answerable to the shareholders of their customers. Indeed, it has been argued that their very presence and involvement with Parmalat gave some reassurance to investors and rating agencies, allowing questionable practices to go unquestioned for longer than they might otherwise. The banks now find themselves at the receiving end, not only of adverse publicity, but of legal action on behalf of the Parmalat administrator. An Italian bank, Banca Intesa, settled early on for an amount of €160m in order to avoid protracted litigation.

Others to suffer reputational damage arising from the Parmalat failure, include rating agencies who continued to issue investment-grade ratings on Parmalat's corporate bonds, despite clear information on its financial status. Even if it could be argued that there was, in fact, a lack of transparency in the publicly reported financial accounts, the expectation would be that creditable rating agencies would delve deeper in order to seek out the truth. When, in fact, it became clear that Parmalat might not be able to repay its debts, the rating agencies acted in haste, slashing the bonds' ratings to junk status, thereby precipitating the company to its ultimate demise.

The case of Parmalat demonstrates that a major corporate failure can result in reputational damage to all parties, directly and indirectly associated with the failure. Individual executives, board members, internal and external auditors, rating agencies, banks and other lenders, as well as the Italian state have all come under criticism for their part in the Parmalat affair. While it will never be possible to eliminate fraudulent behaviour completely, the public, and investors in particular, have a right to expect that those systems put in place to deter, detect and punish wrong-doing, are robust and work in the way they were intended. Enron destroyed the reputations of those that were directly associated with the company, as well as those of its auditors, Andersens. Only time will tell the extent to which Parmalat is Europe's biggest Enron to date.

Lessons learned from Parmalat include the need to:

1. Address the 'spirit' of the law, not just the word of the law

The rotation of auditors and/or the replacement of the main auditing firm after a period of years is intended to ensure a certain level of independence in the auditing process. Auditing partners or firms that retain a connection with their client for many years run the danger of developing too comfortable a relationship with them. This, in turn, may encourage lower levels of scrutiny or, in extreme cases, collaboration with the client in concealing financial information that they would not wish their stakeholders to see. Parmalat was required by Italian law to replace its main auditors, Italaudit, in 1999. They chose not, however, to fully break the connection with a company that had been their long-term auditors. Instead, Italaudit was appointed as auditors to a subsidiary company (Bonlat) that was to play a major role in the alleged fraud that ensued. While the word of the law was addressed, the spirit and intention of the law was undoubtedly not.

2.   Trust your judgment, not that of others

Only a few key players appeared to recognize that something was not quite right with the Parmalat accounts. Others, including major international banks and rating agencies, appear not to have delved deeper into the confused waters surrounding Parmalat's financial transactions, nor to have asked the kind of questions that may have shone some light on the true situation at an earlier stage. This lack of due diligence has led to both financial and reputational loss at well-known global corporations. It is important for both investors and lenders to undertake their own investigations, as far as this is possible, and not to be swayed by the fact that others have been willing to attach their names to, and provide financing for, the company in question.

3.   Beware the 'family friendly' board

Boards that comprise members of the Chairman/CEOs family, and close friends or business partners may be less likely to challenge the strategy or actions of their leader. The failure of Robert Maxwell's Mirror Group Newspapers was, in part, due to an overly compliant board and senior management, in which his two sons played a major role. In such a 'paternalist' board, where the CEO – like Maxwell or Tanzi – is the founder of the firm, as well as its public face, challenge from other board members may be less likely. This, in turn, can lead to serious failures in decision making and, ultimately, to corporate collapse.

4.   Reputation loss has a ripple effect

Corporate failure is rarely, if ever, due to the actions of one person or group of persons. It is generally caused by multiple failures – individual, systems, management – and involves some degree of complicity, either deliberate or by omission, from external parties such as auditors, legal counsel or regulators. Once a company collapses, the ensuing forensic investigation into what went wrong will leave no stone unturned in the process, and will bring into the open every e-mail, memo and document relating to the event. Reputational damage may occur by mere association with the collapsed corporation, even before any tangible evidence of wrongdoing has come into the public domain. In this respect, companies should consider undertaking a strategic risk assessment of their vulnerability to reputation damage, by association with their key clients or customers, and an evaluation of their ability to deal with adverse publicity by means of their crisis management plans.

Postscript

Having read this book, you may feel that much of it has been obvious. You are quite right. On the other hand, when we first began our research we were under the impression that an issue as allegedly difficult as reputational risk would require a series of complex management actions to deal with it. We, like you, quickly changed our opinion. The more we delved into the subject, the more we realised that the individual actions are fairly straightforward and should come as no surprise to any experienced manager.

The real difficulties appear to be in changing the mindset of the organisation. After all, every single employee plays a role that can make or break a reputation. Consequently, there is a battle for hearts and minds that needs to be won. Everyone involved with the organisation must be persuaded that:

a)   the organisation's reputation is immensely valuable;

b)   risk to that reputation is real and is a threat to future viability;

c)   it is in their interests to protect the reputation; and

d)   reputation must be borne in mind whenever they make a decision or come into contact with a stakeholder.

In times past, when command and control cultures still flourished, this might have been easier to achieve. Unfortunately, the ability to implement pan-organisational change easily has been one of the casualties of the more devolved structures in which the great majority of us now work. As a result, much more onus is placed on leadership. In other words, an organisation wishing to manage its reputation will require strong, committed leadership. Are you or your CEO prepared to do it?

Early reactions to the ideas contained in this book

Since we started writing this book, we have had the opportunity to share our conclusions with a large number of people both in seminars and in individual discussion. The response has been overwhelmingly positive but, of course, there has been some push-back. Reputation seems to be one of those subjects on which everyone has emphatic views: no-one seems to remain neutral for long. The strongest support that we received came from more senior management and from those working in the largest organisations. Surprisingly, some of the strongest resistance has come from a small number of practising risk managers.

The negative comments included the following.

◆ The sole purpose of a company is to make money for its shareholders. It owes duties only to shareholders and customers – the only people who put money into the company. Anything given to the public, regulators, employees, or other stakeholders is of minor importance. Those relationships do not need managing.

◆ Reputational risk is too complex an idea. We can't do anything to stop it, so it is not worth trying to manage.

◆ Loss of reputation is not a risk in itself. It is just the consequence of some other risk occurring. It therefore does not need considering in its own right.

◆ We waste enough time and money managing risks. We don't see why we should waste any more on reputational risk management.

On the other hand the positive comments included the following.

◆ The new definition of reputational risk is extremely useful. It helps make the risk more tangible and easier to understand.

◆ The debate about whether reputational risk is a risk in itself or the consequence of other risks is merely semantics.
   The company possesses an asset of (actual or potential) significant value (its reputation). Like all other significant assets that are vital to the company's long-term success, this asset should be effectively managed, protected from damage and, if possible, have its value enhanced.
   Irrespective of what management might think, increasingly regulators and corporate governance rules identify the threat of damage to a company's reputation/reputational risk as a significant, separately identified risk, and expect it to be effectively managed in its own right.

◆ We identify totally with the problem of lack of moral education. We are now finding young people joining the company with very limited understanding of right and wrong. Some have been given very little guidance at home or school. The scary thing is that they are now moving up into management and make decisions on behalf of the company. At one time the purpose of internal controls was to stop the occasional person knowingly breaking the rules. We now are beginning to realise that we may have a need to teach our people about ethics from first principles – it is wrong to: cheat the customer; lie; bully; or act in an unethical or illegal manner.

◆ Our chairman (of a professional services company) has recently come to fully understand the enormous value and importance of the company's reputation and has said that he will support all practical measures that protect it. This has already started to happen. We have been able to establish and properly resource non-fee-earning reputation protection processes that would have been inconceivable before potential reputational loss was factored into the cost benefit analysis.

◆ The organisation's reputation must be owned by the CEO or chairman and then the importance of protecting and growing the reputation embedded throughout the culture of the organisation from the very top to the bottom. How this is done will depend on the culture of the organisation and the management style of the 'owner'.

Reputation management should not be someone else's job, or an additional bureaucracy or process, it should be part of what every employee does in performing their roles on a daily basis.

◆ It's common sense. It is just systematically applying, to the large and complex organisation, the principles that the proprietor of a small business would find intuitive and use informally.

Appendix I

An extract from:
An Interfaith Declaration:
A code of ethics on international
business for Christians, Muslims
and Jews

Guidelines

1. Business and political economy

All business activity takes place within the context of a social, political and economic system. It is recognised that:

a.   Business is part of the social order. Its primary purpose is to meet human and material needs by producing and distributing goods and services in an efficient manner. How this role is carried out – the means as well as the ends – is important to society.

b.   Competition between businesses has generally been shown to be the most effective way to ensure that resources are not wasted, costs are minimised and prices fair. The state has a duty to see that markets operate effectively, competition is maintained and natural monopolies are regulated. Business will not seek to frustrate this.

c.   All economic systems have flaws; that based on free and open markets is morally neutral and has great potential for good. Private enterprise sometimes has the potential to make efficient and sustainable use of resources, thereby creating wealth which can be used for the benefit of everyone.

d. There is no basic conflict between good business practice and profit making. Profit is one measure of efficiency and is of paramount importance in the functioning of the system. It provides for the maintenance and growth of business, thus expanding employment opportunities, and is the means of a rising living standard for all concerned. It also acts as an incentive to work and be enterprising. It is from the profit of companies that society can reasonably levy taxes to finance its wider needs.

e. Because the free market system, like any other, is open to abuse, it can be used for selfish or sectional interests, or it can be used for good. The state has an obligation to provide a framework of law in which business can operate honestly and fairly and business will obey and respect the law of the state in which it operates.

f. As business is a partnership of people of varying gifts they should never be considered as merely factors of production. The terms of their employment will be consistent with the highest standards of human dignity.

g. The efficient use of scarce resources will be ensured by the business. Resources employed by corporations include finance (savings), technology (machinery) and land and natural renewable resources. All are important and most are scarce.

h. Business has a responsibility to future generations to improve the quality of goods and services, not to degrade the natural environment in which it operates, and seek to enrich the lives of those who work within it. Short-term profitability should not be pursued at the expense of long-term viability of the business. Neither should business operations disadvantage the wider community.

2   The policies of a business

Business activity involves human relationships. It is the question of balancing the reasonable interests of those involved in the process, ie the stakeholders, that produces moral and ethical problems.

The policies of the business will therefore be based on the principles set out in the paragraphs above (ie *justice, mutual respect, stewardship, honesty*) and in particular:

a. The board of directors will be responsible for seeing that the business operates within the letter and spirit of the laws of the nations in which it works. If these laws are rather less rigorous in some parts of the world where the business operates than in others, the higher standards will normally be applied everywhere.

b. The board will issue a written statement concerning the objectives and operating policies of the organisation and their application. It will set out clearly the obligations of the company towards the different stakeholders involved with a business (employees, lenders, customers, suppliers and the community (local and national government)).

c. The basis of the relationship with the principal stakeholders shall be honesty and fairness, by which is meant integrity, in all relationships, as well as reliability in all commitments made on behalf of the organisation.

d. The business shall maintain a continuing relationship with each of the groups with which it is involved. It will provide effective means to communicate information affecting the stakeholders. This relationship is based on trust.

e. The best practice to be adopted in dealings with six particular stakeholders can be summarised as follows:

 i. Employees

 Employees make a unique contribution to an organisation; it follows that in their policies businesses shall, where appropriate, take notice of trade union positions and provide:

 - working conditions that are safe and healthy and conducive to high standards of work;

 - levels of remuneration that are fair and just, that recognise the employees' contribution to the organisation and the performance of the sector of the business in which they work;

 - a respect for the individual (whether male or female) in their beliefs, their family responsibility and their need to grow as human beings. It will provide equal opportunities in training and promotion for all members of the organisation. It will not discriminate in its policies on grounds of race, colour, creed, or gender.

 ii. Providers of finance

 A business cannot operate without finance. There is, therefore, a partnership between the provider and the user. The company borrowing the money shall give to the lender:

 - What has been agreed to be repaid at the due dates.

 - Adequate safeguards in using the resources entrusted.

 - Regular information of the operations of the business and opportunities to raise with directors matters concerning their performance.

 iii. Customers

 Without customers a business cannot survive. In selling products or services, a company shall provide for the customer:

- The quality and standard of service which has been agreed.
- After-sales service commensurate with the type of product or service and the price paid.
- Where applicable, a contract written in unambiguous terms.
- Informative and accurate information regarding the use of the product or service especially where misuse can be dangerous.

iv.   Suppliers

Suppliers provide a daily flow of raw materials, products and services to enable a business to operate. The relationship with suppliers is normally a long-term one and must therefore be based on mutual trust. The company shall:

- Undertake to pay its suppliers promptly and in accordance with agreed terms of trade.
- Not use its buying power in an unscrupulous fashion.
- Require buyers to report offers of gifts, favours of unusual size or questionable purpose.

v.   Community (local and national government)

While companies have an obligation to work within the law, they must also take into account the effects of their activities on local and national communities. In particular they shall:

- ensure that they protect the local environment from harmful emissions from manufacturing plant, excessive noise and any practice likely to endanger humans, animals or plant life;
- consider the social consequences of company decisions eg plant closures, choice of any new sites or expansion of existing ones, and the effects on smaller businesses;
- not tolerate any form of bribery, extortion or other corrupt practices in business dealings.

vi.   Owners (shareholders)

The shareholders undertake the risks of ownership. The elected directors shall:

- protect the interests of shareholders;
- see that the company's accounting statements are true and timely;

- see that shareholders are kept informed of all major happenings affecting the company.

3. Conduct of individuals at work

The following are based on best ethical practice for employees in a business. Employees in an organisation shall:

a. implement the decisions of those to whom he or she is responsible which are lawful and in accordance with the company's policies, in co-operation with colleagues;

b. avoid all abuse of power for personal gain, advantage or prestige, and in particular refuse bribes or other inducements of any sort intended to encourage dishonesty or to break the law;

c. not use any information acquired in the business for personal gain or for the benefit of relatives or outside associates;

d. reveal the facts to his superiors whenever his personal business or financial interests become involved with those of the company;

e. be actively concerned with the difficulties and problems of subordinates, treat them fairly and lead them effectively, assuring them a right of reasonable access and appeal to those to whom their immediate superior is responsible;

f. bring to the attention of superiors the likely effects on employees of the company's plans for the future so that such effects can be fully taken into account.

Appendix 2

Developing a code of ethics/ ethical best practice

If you will excuse the irony, there is no absolute, right way or wrong way to develop a code of ethics/ethical best practice. Nevertheless, having helped to introduce several codes, and seen many more in action, we suggest that the following factors should be considered by anyone contemplating undertaking the task. Some of the factors were originally inspired by the Institute of Business Ethics who gave us some excellent advice when we wrote our first code a decade ago.

(a) **High level sponsorship**
The process should be seen to have the personal support of the Chief Executive to demonstrate its importance and permanence.

(b) **Strong leadership**
The actual work should be led by a manager of considerable drive and credibility to ensure that the thinking is rigorous, sensitive issues are not avoided, and the process is driven through the entire organisation.

(c) **Teamwork**
The leader should be supported by a team that consults widely inside the company and researches best practice from outside.

(d) **Ethical values**
The logical starting point is the company's basic values which might include honesty, openness, integrity, fairness, respect for human rights and the law, but should also be linked to the reasonable expectations of all stakeholders.

Keeping promises

We will promise only what we expect to deliver, make only commitments we intend to keep, not knowingly mislead others, and not participate in or condone corrupt or unacceptable business practices.
Extract – BP Business Policy, Ethical Conduct

(e) **Strategic objectives**

Another input might be the company's strategic objectives. To ensure that the strategy and behaviour are aligned, the question might be asked, 'What behaviours are required to facilitate achievement of the strategic objectives?'

(f) **Board approval**

The code should be signed off by the board as company policy.

(g) **Communication**

The code should be put into easily communicable forms and given to the employees and other stakeholders where appropriate. Sanctions for non-compliance and arrangements for whistle blowing should be explained. Where possible the code should be made part of employees' contracts of employment.

(h) **Training**

All those affected by the code should be trained in its use and when to seek advice. Even well thought out ethical codes may fail to produce the desired standards of behaviour if they are not embedded in the organisation. Some companies treat them merely as PR exercises, some forget them as soon as they are written (another box ticked) and some have been known to not even have communicated them to their employees.

(i) **Implementation**

Processes and structures should be set up, both to implement the code, and operate it on a day-to-day basis, that are, as far as possible, simple, effective and non-bureaucratic. Performance measures and benchmarks should be incorporated within these processes for all areas of performance that are deemed critical to meeting key stakeholder expectations.

Codes of conduct

Having a code of conduct is not, however, enough. It can only be effective and practically useful with committed dissemination, implementation, monitoring and embedding at all levels so that behaviour is influenced.

Institute of Business Ethics, www.ibe.org.uk

(j) **Monitoring**

Compliance should be monitored. (Some companies publish details of the results of their ethical behaviour monitoring processes.)

(k) **Updating**

The code should be regularly reviewed and updated as necessary. (Stakeholder perceptions of ethical best practice can and do change over time.)

Good examples of codes produced by companies are those of Unilever, BP, Cadbury Schweppes and Diageo, all of which can be accessed via their websites.

Unilever's Code of Business Principles

- Unilever's Code of Business Principles sets out its principles relating to employees, consumers, shareholders, business partners, the wider community and government bodies. It states Unilever's ethical position on the environment, innovation and competition, and on the business dealings of the company and its employees. It sets out how these commitments are upheld, maintained and managed from day to day.

- 'We conduct our operations with honesty, integrity and openness, and with respect for the human rights and interests of our employees.' Extract from the Code

- 'All our business plans are always written on the implicit understanding that the Code of Business Principles must be adhered to.' Antony Burgmans, Joint Chairman

- Any company can choose fine-sounding words like 'integrity' and 'respect', but it means little if management and employees do not follow these principles. Unilever is committed to ensuring that its Code lives within the company and permeates its business.

- Unilever is duty bound to show that it is a good neighbour and employer in the communities where it operates.

- The Code is, in effect, Unilever's 'contract' with society. It sets out the standards by which the company interacts with society. And because Unilever lives through its employees, the Code is also their 'contract' with the business and the wider society in which they work and live.

- It is the responsibility of every Unilever person to maintain and safeguard Unilever's corporate reputation.

Extracted from an article in Unilever's in-house magazine introducing the revised Unilever Code of Business Principles, 2003

Appendix 3

Making it happen: Practical considerations in implementing the reputational risk management process

1. CEO to assume responsibility for reputation

In a small company the proprietor would automatically take responsibility for the organisation's reputation. Indeed, he or she would probably identify it closely with their own personal reputation.

- ◆ Should this situation be any different in a larger organisation?
- ◆ Who actually takes the responsibility in your organisation?
- ◆ If a major problem did occur would the CEO's personal reputation be tarnished?

2. Assign responsibility for the reputational risk management process

The senior executive given this responsibility should be chosen with sensitivity. Other managers could easily regard this as an appointment to second guess what they do in their own areas. Buy-in is essential.

- ◆ Who in your organisation would have the credibility and skills to maintain the co-operation of colleagues and carry the process through to a successful conclusion?

◆ Could they do it alone or would they need the help of external consultants or an ad hoc internal team?

3. Understand the value of your reputation

Placing a value on your organisation's reputation is not an exact science, but having a rough idea will be helpful in deciding how much effort needs to be placed on its management and also in obtaining buy-in to the overall process. In some cases the value can be a multiple of the physical asset value.

◆ Could you estimate the monetary value of the reputation of your organisation?
◆ Could you estimate the non-financial value of the reputation of your organisation?
◆ How does its 'value' compare with the current management effort devoted to reputational management?

4. Understand the stakeholder expectations

Our definition of reputational risk, which is centred on failure to satisfy stakeholder expectations, leads to the obvious question: have organisations taken the trouble to identify those expectations? It is likely that they will have a reasonable idea of what customers and shareholders expect, but many organisations might have to struggle somewhat harder to articulate exactly what employees, regulators, business partners, the public and relevant NGOs want.

◆ How easily could you list the real (as opposed to the assumed) expectations of each of your stakeholder groups?
◆ Are you able to clearly demonstrate to what extent you currently satisfy each set of stakeholder expectations?

5. Determine company policy

This is likely to be a very illuminating debate in a management team. They might learn some very interesting things about their colleagues' approach to business and even their personal philosophies.

◆ Do you believe that your top team currently share the same views on how business should be conducted?
◆ If not, would the organisation be willing to compromise its principles, or would it have to change the team?

6.   Identify all significant causes of reputational risk

This could easily be undertaken by desk research, but it might be better to use a brainstorming workshop involving people selected from various parts of the organisation. Not only could this give a wider perspective, but it could assist in improving overall awareness among staff. Consultants can be especially useful at this stage as they can provide input from their own experience as well as running workshops.

◆ Who in your organisation would contribute most to the identification exercise?

7.   Prioritise

The value of identifying the most important causes in terms of probability and impact is that it forms a basis for management priorities.

◆ Could you list the top five potential causes of reputational risk for your company?
◆ Do you think that the senior and middle managers would agree with your assessment?
◆ Why might they not agree with you, or with each other?

8.   Identify appropriate control activity for each cause of risk

The introduction of ethical best practice into an organisation might well emerge as an appropriate control procedure. This is likely to be effective only if it is fully accepted and implemented by the whole workforce.

◆ Would ethical best practice represent a culture shock to your organisation?
◆ How easily could it be embedded?
◆ Where would you anticipate the strongest resistance to arise?

9.   Implement reputational risk management controls and integrate with other risk management activity

Those causes of risk and controls that do not neatly fall into other organisational processes might need careful consideration.

◆ Do any of the priorities identified above fall into the orphan category?
◆ How might they be implemented?

10. Review as a single risk

The last thing we would be advocating is that reputational risk management should require a new bureaucracy of its own. Once the necessary controls have been identified they should be taken up by the existing organisation. However, the information should not be lost. This is particularly important if the organisation is to be able to prove to the relevant authorities, auditors, etc that it has identified and is controlling all of its major risks.

◆ Could your organisation prove to an outsider that it is managing the entirety of its reputational risk in an effective and appropriate manner?

11. Alignment with strategic objectives and organisational performance measures

Once a proper understanding of the organisation's actual and desired reputation, and the risks to that reputation, has been achieved, and decisions made as to how the reputation can be managed/enhanced/protected, the organisation will need to look at the existing strategic objectives to ensure that there is complete and unambiguous alignment between the two. If reputational risk management requires additional consideration to be paid to stakeholders other than shareholders or customers, or a focus on long-term shareholder value maximisation as opposed to short-term, this must not conflict with the organisation's strategic objectives. In certain circumstances the strategic objectives may need to be reworded/adjusted in the light of the better understanding of the value of the organisation's reputation.

Similarly, the performance and behaviour standards, measures and incentives in place within the organisation may need to be adjusted to reflect the desired approach to reputational risk management (eg incentive schemes that encourage behaviour that may negatively impact on the organisation's reputation).

◆ Are your organisation's strategic objectives and performance and behaviour measures fully consistent with the concept of protecting and enhancing the organisation's reputation in its broadest sense?

Appendix 4

Example of an active risk management approach, from specialist reputational risk consultants Brotzen Mayne

Reputation risk: best practices

- Reputation risk review

- Reputation risk map

- Action plan for 'top 5' risks

- Reputation risk integrated in risk strategy

- Training/simulations

- System to monitor and assess risk

- Escalation plan

- Trained crisis team

- Crisis manual/intranet

- Review process

BROTZEN
MAYNE
LIMITED

©Brotzen Mayne Ltd. March 2003

Appendix 5

Example of a reputational risk management process: FTSE 100 company

1. The corporate reputation is regarded as being of great importance to the group.

2. Ownership of the corporate reputation is acknowledged by the CEO in a statement of policy.

3. Responsibility for oversight and co-ordination of reputational risk management is vested in the Group Risk Director.

4. Implementation of controls is then via the normal operational management processes and functional policies (HR, H&S, CSR, etc). There are particularly active corporate communications and investor relations teams.

5. Reputation is considered to depend on maintaining a variety of stakeholder relationships (eg employees, customers, government, suppliers, society), but the shareholder relationship has the top priority,

6. Reputational risk is a central part of the company's operational risk. A report by the Group Risk Director on progress in its management and issues arising is a standard agenda item at each monthly board meeting.

7. The value of the reputation is regularly monitored by a variety of methods including press favourability scoring.

8. Education of all management of the importance of reputation and the impact of their behaviour is essential.

9. There is a pyramid of balanced scorecards where stakeholder requirements are translated into individual management and company targets. No manager is given a bonus unless all his/her stakeholder targets are reached.

10. There is a stakeholder review in the report and accounts describing the state of each stakeholder relationship.

Appendix 6

Managing reputation in a crisis

When we interviewed Julia Graham of the Business Continuity Institute, she explained the inter-relationship between risk management, continuity management and reputation. Placing it in its historical context, she said:

> Ten years ago if you had picked up this book you probably would have been a marketing or communications manager. The concept of managing reputation was, and still is, to a significant degree, off-line to the management agenda generally, and to risk and business continuity management specifically. But today, if it is accepted that reputation can add value to an organisation and form a measurable asset on the balance sheet, then just as surely can a poorly managed crisis reduce the value of reputation equity.
>
> In the early 1990s board-level interest in risk management and internal controls was largely focussed on financial and treasury issues and, whilst there were some organisations that took a wide-angle view of risk and controls beyond finance, even in these cases, attention was generally focussed on hazard-related or insurable risk. With broad insurance coverage at highly competitive prices freely available a decade ago, there were very few reasons for 'insurable risk' to be brought out of daily financial management and to the attention of the board. Many risk commentators mark the terrible events of September 2001 as the date this all changed, but the roots of modern risk and business continuity management are older and were already becoming deeply embedded in organisational management long before that fateful day in 2001.

" There are numerous surveys of managers addressing the question of what risks keep them awake at night. These surveys indicate that organisations are increasing in their desire to investigate how they might manage all risks across their business, coupled with a growing division in management priorities and approach between managing the more predictable and quantifiable risks, and the unforeseeable and more intangible risks. Further, business continuity management, so long a subject in the domain of the information technology department, continues to attract wider interest as a potential capability for building the overall resilience of an organisation, and as a key control and mechanism for risk mitigation complementary to transfer of risk by insurance.

Three interesting features, common to most surveys are: a perceptible escalation of the intangible risks in the league tables of risk concerns at the expense of the more tangible, quantifiable and transferable risks; continuing concern over the risks that are difficult to predict and consequently to plan for; and, that aggregation and domino effects on organisations are rising in an increasingly interdependent and global business world.

There has been a growing realisation that organisations need to manage all risks, both tangible and intangible, and business continuity management must rise to the challenge to respond. The silos of risk management are being drawn closer together into an integrated enterprise risk management framework. Whether the drivers for change are internal to an organisation, or external through governance, regulatory or legislative pressures, risk management and business continuity management have come of age as united disciplines. If an organisation is to effectively address the above issues then business continuity management must form part of the organisation's risk management, corporate governance and quality management systems.

In the modern business, business continuity management is an enterprise-wide professional discipline embracing all strategic and operational aspects of an organisation: contributing to business resilience and long-term business performance both during times of normality as well as times of extreme and unplanned response. The outcomes of business continuity management today need to contribute a substantial benefit to the continuity of an organisation before a major disruption, as well as following the disruption. Large organisations are not immune from large incidents and senior management should ask themselves not only how reputation can contribute to value, but how a crisis can impact reputation and value – and consequently how they would respond in a reputation-threatening scenario. "

> Managing the impact of a crisis is part of good management practice; managed well, an incident can add value to an organisation, managed badly, the result may be terminal and management may not see the business recover sufficiently to experience the learning of how otherwise they might have performed more effectively.

The practical aspects of actually managing a crisis were graphically described to us by Linda Lewis. She has been able to approach the subject from 'the opposite side of the fence' as, for 20 years, she was a national television reporter and presenter for BBC News. Her work has taken her to many crises, and she has experienced first hand the best and worst of corporate responses. She now runs a communications consultancy, Lewis New Media, providing online and new media training and communication tools, along with face-to-face coaching in media handling and interview skills. Her website www.e-mergencyonline.com makes fascinating browsing. She writes:

> Anyone who has to manage a crisis or a serious incident will find their resources put severely to the test. Dealing with the communication aspects is likely to push those resources, especially human ones, to the very limit. If you are unprepared for the intensity of the likely media scrutiny or if — a cardinal sin — you allow a communication vacuum to develop in the first few, crucial hours as an incident unfolds — then you risk creating the impression that you either do not know, or do not care, what is going on. Either way, once a company or organisation's image has been tarnished, restoring credibility is much harder than protecting it properly in the first place.
>
> In today's 24/7 global media world, bad news travels just as fast as it takes to jack up a satellite news feed, or to propel a reporter into a studio breathlessly relating the 'latest' as gleaned by rapid scanning of the agency wires and a few hurried phone calls. The first reports of any incident are always sketchy, relying as they do on eyewitness testimony. There is a dearth of facts, and news-gatherers' urgent priority is to get reporters, camera crews, 'fixers', links vehicles, OB units and photographers to the site of the incident as quickly as possible and 'go live' from the scene. 24-hour news programming requires constant feeding and updating, which places a huge amount of pressure on those in front of the camera (and denies them, some would argue, the chance to engage in real reporting, as opposed to 'instant video-packaging' and speculation).

“ As part of a pro-active communications strategy, you need to ensure an equally rapid response, first of all by issuing a holding statement giving the facts as you have been able to establish them so far. You also need to have procedures in place, usually as part of a crisis management plan, to handle the media's demands for interviews, background briefings, company statistics, permission for access, and — a sad but necessary duty to protect families of the victims — photographs of and tributes to any staff members killed or injured in an incident.

Your website offers an additional communication channel, allowing you to talk directly to stakeholders and the public at large without having to run the gauntlet of journalists firing questions. Increasingly, people are using the internet as their primary source of information in a crisis. Campaign groups, such as animal activists and environmentalists, have been quick to exploit the communication potential of the internet, eg by incorporating email petitions and powerful multimedia material such as interviews and videos into their websites. By comparison, many corporate sites are left wanting — characterised as they are by dull, boring, lengthy column inches of text, laden with technical gobbledygook and inflexible content management systems.

All too often, it seems, websites are a bolt-on, a secondary consideration, when in my view they are a vastly under-used communication resource. Potentially, they offer any company or organisation in the public eye the chance to be their own TV or radio station, to tell their side of the story and get over key messages without risk of being edited, dropped or annihilated by an over-aggressive interviewer. Most importantly, in the prevailing 'guilty until proven innocent' media culture, they allow those whose reputation is on the line to show their human face, and demonstrate in a visible, accountable and caring way, how they are dealing with an incident, not least its impact on people.

By practising 'joined-up communication' it is possible to make highly effective use of your website as a reputation protection tool. IT, PR and BC professionals working together can consolidate three elements of reputational risk: how-to-do-it, how-to-say-it and how-to-manage it. Progressive corporate communications departments are starting to realise this. However, it often requires a catalyst to bring these three distinct divisions of many organisations together, which is where consultants can be useful. Digital technology has brought huge changes for broadcasters. Used imaginatively, it can also bring huge changes to those subjected to media exposure who wish to take control of their own communication, and protect one of their most precious assets. ”

Appendix 7

Bibliography and useful websites

Reputation

Alsop, R.J. (2004) *The 18 Immutable Laws of Corporate Reputation*, London: Kogan Page

Knight, R.F. and Pretty, D.J. (2001) *Reputation and Value: The Case of Corporate Catastrophes*, Oxford: Oxford Metrica

Reputational Risk

Griffin, G. (2002) *Reputation Management*, Oxford: Capstone Publishing.

Larkin, J. (2003) *Strategic Reputation Risk Management*, Basingstoke: Palgrave MacMillan.

Neef, D. (2003) *Managing Corporate Reputation and Risk: A Strategic Approach Using Knowledge Management*, Burlington MA: Elsevier Butterworth Heinemann

Rayner, J. (2001) *Risky Business: Towards Best Practice in Managing Reputation Risk*, London: Institute of Business Ethics

Rayner, J. (2003) *Managing Reputational Risk*, Chichester: John Wiley & Sons.

Corporate behaviour

Bakan, J. (2004) *The Corporation*, Constable & Robinson

Cowe, R. (2002) *No Scruples*, Spiro Press

HIH Royal Commission (2001), www.hihroyalcom.gov.au

Mitchell, L. (2000) *Corporate Irresponsibility*, Yale University Press

A New Vision for Business, UK Government Committee of Inquiry, 1999

Nixon, B. (2001) *Global Forces*, Management Books 2000 Ltd

Pettinger, R. (2002) *Global Organisations*, Capstone Publishing

Corporate social responsibility

Association of British Insurers (2000) *Investing in Corporate Responsibility*, London: ABI

Harvard Business Review on Corporate Responsibility (2003) Boston: Harvard Business School Publishing

Schwartz, P. and Gibb, B. (1999) *When Good Companies Do Bad Things*, New York: John Wiley & Sons

Business ethics

Harvard Business Review on Corporate Ethics (2003) Boston: Harvard Business School Publishing

Megone, C. and Robinson, S.J. [eds.] (2002) *Case Histories in Business Ethics*

Webley, S. and Le Jeune, M. (2002) *Ethical Business: Corporate Use of Codes of Conduct*, London: Institute of Business Ethics

Webley, S. and More, E. (2003) *Does Business Ethics Pay?*, London: Institute of Business Ethics

Webley, S. (2003) *Developing a Code of Business Ethics*, London: Institute of Business Ethics

Corporate governance

Cadbury, A. (2002) *Corporate Governance and Chairmanship: A Personal View*, Oxford: Oxford University Press

Coyle, B. (2002) *Risk Awareness and Corporate Governance*, Canterbury: Financial World Publishing

MacAvoy, P.W. and Millstein, I.M. (2003) *The Recurrent Crisis in Corporate Governance*, Basingstoke: Palgrave MacMillan

Mallin, C.A. (2004), *Corporate Governance*, Oxford: Oxford University Press

Shaw, J.C. (2003) *Corporate Governance and Risk: A Systems Approach*, New Jersey: John Wiley & Sons

Sternberg, E. (2004) *Corporate Governance: Accountability in the Marketplace*, London: Institute of Economic Affairs

Risk management

Hopkin, P. (2002) *Holistic Risk Management in Practice*, London: Witherby & Co.

Jeynes, J. (2002) *Risk Management: 10 Principles*, Oxford: Butterworth Heinemann

Waring A. and Glendon, A.I. (1998) *Managing Risk: Critical Issues for Survival and Success Into the 21st Century*, London: International Thomson Business Press

Young, P.C. and Tippins, S.C. (2001) *Managing Business Risk: An Organization-Wide Approach to Risk Management*, New York: Amacom

Crisis management

Harvard Business Review on Crisis Management (2000) Boston: Harvard Business School Press

Mitroff, I.A. (2001) *Managing Crises Before They Happen;* New York: Amacom

Regester, M. and Larkin, J. (2002) *Risk Issues and Crisis Management* 2nd edition, London: Kogan Page

Seymour, M. and Moore, S. (2000) *Effective Crisis Management: Worldwide Principles and Practice*, London: Cassell

Miscellaneous

Cruver, B. (2002) *Anatomy of Greed*, London: Hutchinson

Elliot, A.L. and Schroth, R.J. (2002) *How Companies Lie: Why Enron Is Just The Tip Of The Iceberg*, London: Nicholas Brealey Publishing

Fox, L. (2003) *Enron: The Rise and Fall*, New Jersey: John Wiley & Sons

Jeter, L. W. (2003) *Disconnected: Deceit And Betrayal At WorldCom*, New Jersey: John Wiley & Sons

Gladwell, M. (2000) *The Tipping Point*, Abacus

Harvard Business Review on Measuring Corporate Performance (1998) Boston: Harvard Business School Publishing

Paxman, J. (2002) *The Political Animal*, Michael Joseph, Penguin Group

Vaughan, D. (1996) *The Challenger Launch Decision: Risky Technology, Culture and Deviance at NASA*, Chicago: The Universityof Chicago Press

Useful websites

Reputational risk consultants

www.aon.co.uk
www.brotzen-mayne.co.uk
www.marsh.com
www.willis.co.uk

Crisis communications

www.e-mergencyonline.com

Corporate behaviour consultants

www.kaisen.co.uk
www.rogersteare.com

Institutions

Association of British Insurers   www.abi.org.uk

Association of Insurance and Risk Managers in Commerce   www.airmic.com

Glasgow Caledonian University Centre for Risk and Governance
 www.caledoniancrag.com

Institute of Business Ethics   www.ibe.org.uk

Institute of Financial Services   www.ifslearning.com

Institute of Risk Management   www.theirm.org

Business Continuity Institute www.thebci.org

Index